Self Publishing Your Way Now

Earma Brown

Self-Publishing Your Way Now!

How to *Publish to Profit* Your Book, Your Way Now

DEDICATION

I dedicate *Self Publishing Your Way Now* to my sisters: Oneadia
Kates, Marie Toms, Cecelia Tasby, Marilyn Worsham,
Linda Howard, Minnie Broadway

CONTENTS

ACKNOWLEDGMENTS

A big thank you to my husband Varn Brown
for his support and partnership.

INTRODUCTION

DESIGNING YOUR OWN PUBLISHING OPPORTUNITIES!

Today, more than ever before, is the age of information. Twenty-four hours a day, seven days a week, there continues to be an incredible demand for information throughout America and the world. There is an astronomical demand for information packed books, manuals, reports and newsletters of almost every imaginable kind.

It's really much easier than you might have ever guessed to start filling your bank account with cash from information you possess. People crave information that appeals to their basic needs and will somehow educate or enlighten them. Simply by putting your own specialized information into books, manuals, reports or newsletters, you can start putting a hefty price on information you have no doubt been giving away.

This book details the growing method with which authors and publishers alike can use self-publishing and/or publish-on-demand (POD) services to cut costs and increase profits, while reaching new readers through the new millennium cash pot of Internet marketing.

Publishers Marketing Association estimates there are 73,000 small and self- publishers in the U.S., with 8,000-11,000 new ones each year

- Of the approximately 2.8 million books in print, 78% of the titles come from small/self-publishers (PMA)

- For small and self-publishers, sales increased 21% annually from 1997-2002; in 2002, these 73,000 publishers grossed $29.4 billion

- 81% of the population feels they have a book inside them; 6 million have written a manuscript; and another 6 million have a manuscript making the rounds. You become a "self-publisher" by taking your material (book, manual, report, newsletter, etc.) and by-pass all the middlemen.

You by-pass the middlemen, by going directly to a printer and handling all the marketing and distribution of the product yourself. As a self-publisher you invest your talent, time and energy and money. The benefits you receive are complete control over your product and all the profits.

HERE ARE TEN GOOD REASONS TO SELF-PUBLISH:

1. *Self-publishing may be the only way to get published.* With thousands upon thousands of manuscripts and more sent to publishers continually you may not be able to get to anyone to even look at your idea. Self-publishing may be your only solution.

2. As a self-publisher *you get to keep all of the profits from your sales.* Why accept 4-5-6% in royalties from a publishing company when you can have it all!

3. *You have absolute marketing and editing control when you self-publish.* According to A Writer's Digest poll, 60% of the traditional publishing firms do the final editing; 23% select the final title; 20% will not even consult an author on the cover design, and 37% do not involve authors in promoting their own material.

4. Major publishers may receive up to several hundred manuscripts a week. Unless they have already published your work, the odds *they will even look at your material aren't very high.*

5. *When you self-publish you are in control every step of the way.* By depending on another publisher to make things

happen for you, you take the chance of never getting anywhere.

6. By self-publishing *you gain the perspective of being able to see the complete marketing picture* from a publisher's point of view.

7. Even if a publisher did accept your work, *it would take an average of 18 months before the first copy reached the marketplace.*

8. *Self-publishing will save you valuable time.* Especially if you can't afford to miss a market that can quickly pass by.

9. Waiting for a letter from a publisher that never comes can be frustrating and embarrassing. *Self-publishing eliminates the waiting and wondering.* When you self-publish and get more directly involved in marketing you will obtain a more total business picture.

10. As a self-publisher *you will receive more tax advantages.*

SUMMARY

Think about it if you don't pursue your dream now; you may be this time next year still wondering about your book dream. You can make a lot of money by writing and self-publishing your own book, if you are willing to invest the time into a book that millions of people across the United States, and throughout the world for that matter, desperately want to buy.

Chapter 1

SEVEN STEP PROGRAM TO WRITE YOUR BOOK NOW!

Anyone can write a book filled with their passionate information, message or expertise. Yet many do not because they assume they aren't talented enough, they don't have the time, it won't sell, it will take too long or it won't be significant.

Are you one of those who delay assuming it won't work for various reasons? Imagine for a moment that all of those assumptions and concerns could be dissolved and an easy plan emerged that would help you get your book written and out to help the world.

WHAT IF EVERYONE COULD WRITE A BOOK?

What if everyone that wanted to write a book could do so easily? Now you can with "Write Your Best Book Now" program with seven easy steps that will help you profit from your passion. With these seven steps you can establish yourself as an authority, create multiple income streams and promote your insightful message and expertise. Here's an overview of the seven steps covered in this book. Implement these and profit from your passions whatever they may be:

1. *Start with a plan to pursue your goal and win.*

Your WIN is the successful completion of your book marketed to a targeted audience with more book sales than you dreamed. Your map is a written marketing plan including the goal, the route and passion points (signs) along the way. Our 7 step writing program is your vehicle of choice to take you to your goal.

Starting your journey with a written marketing plan will guide you down your book path with ease and direction. Also, authors who enjoy the greatest success work from a plan even a program that begins with a book. The book is the beginning not the end. The *Write Your Best Book Now* program helps you describe your book, the characteristics of its market including who and why they will buy it.

> "Your WIN is the successful completion of your book marketed to a targeted audience with more book sales than you dreamed."

Developing your book following the program explains how you will build upon the credibility and visibility your book creates. Your plan will describe how you will promote your book as well as develop multiple streams of income from it.

Following this plan, encourages you to view your book as an expandable "concept" instead of just one title. It will encourage you to build a structure and insert modules of your existing information into it resulting in easy, step by step writing of a successful book(s).

Begin by asking some fundamental marketing questions: Who is your target audience, who do you want to buy your book, what problems do they face, what motivates them (fear, anger), why will they buy your book, what benefit will your book offer its readers, what will you do to promote your book and ways you can profit from your book's success.

2. *Setup passion points to guide your book to success.*

Every part should be written passionately and designed to be a sales tool. Touch your readers' emotion with passion for your topic and you'll sell more books. In fact, when you design your book to include the passion points below, you'll sell more books than you ever imagined.

Your first passion point should be to write to help one targeted audience. It's true your book won't interest everyone. But there is a community of people in your field waiting for you to solve their problem. What problems does your message solve for them?

Secondly, but just as importantly sizzle your title and book cover as passion points. Researchers say you have around 20 seconds to hook your potential buyer including front and back covers. An excellent title is short. The top titles are benefit driven. Don't forget to heat them up with emotion.

Devise your theme as one central thought. Best sellers focus on one theme. It makes your copy more focused and compelling than it would be otherwise. Design your mini-billboard or your 30 second commercial for elevators, grocery lines and anywhere you have only a few seconds to tell and sell.

> "Researchers say you have around 20 seconds to hook your potential buyer including front and back covers."

Your back cover is another important passion point that should be designed to sell. It should be written as a mini-sales letter driven by benefits for your reader as well. Write your back cover before you write your book.

Develop your introduction. State the problem your reader has, why you wrote the book, and its purpose. Compile a table of contents including sizzling chapter titles. If the chapter titles are not obvious, then annotate them. Don't forget to begin early to contact influencers in your field. These experienced contacts' testimonials will lend influence to your back cover making it a powerful sales tool.

3. *Sizzle your titles with passion to sell more.*

Create sizzling titles designed to hook your potential readers. One of the most important skills to develop as a marketer of your book is the skill of creating attention-grabbing titles. When you master this skill you may use it in every aspect of your writing to attract more readers, more sales, improve your cash flow and increase your profits.

> "If you don't want your marketing messages to be lost in the sea of information streaming into your reader's consciousness each day, you must title them well."

You will need title writing skill for your book titles, chapter titles, sub-heading. Even bullet points will have pulling power if they are developed correctly. Your website will need passionate headings to capture the attention of your web visitors.

If you don't want your marketing messages to be lost in the sea of information streaming into your reader's consciousness each day, you must title them well. In fact, any marketing material from your 5 page sales letter or tri-fold brochure to the 2 line classified ad needs the attention grabbing power of a great headline.

Titles set the stage for your potential audience. They either will work to grab your potential reader by the collar and pull them in for the read or they don't. Top titles create excitement, anticipation and enthusiasm for more. You want your titles to express the heart and passion of your message or be 'the match' that ignites your reader's interest in reading your important message.

Develop this valuable skill and you add magnetic pulling power and punch to all your marketing documents including your front book cover and chapter titles that will get your message read.

4. *Mine your knowledge like gold.*

One of the main concepts of the 7 step writing program of the *Write Your Best Book Now* book includes excavating your unique groups of existing knowledge and opinions. Many people think they have to be super smart while doing tons of research on a topic they barely know anything about much less feel any passion for.

Following this program you will put out modules or nuggets from existing information from your speeches, classes, articles, brochures. If you've never done this before, you may be surprised at what turns up.

When you organize your information into groups and categories, it will be easier to write your book and easier to repackage your ideas into newsletters, articles, speeches and website reports that will help market and sell your book.

These nugget ideas in its various forms will engage your readers and build your creditability. With anything valuable such as gold, the sifting process will reveal the rough cut form (draft). Then a process called refining is used where heat is applied to purify and even re-shape and polish the gold to its fullest potential.

So it is with your collection of knowledge and experiences. Sift through your files and memories looking for nuggets (groups of pertinent information) you can identify, organize and write about. Then apply the heat of purging unnecessary information. Burn away all the dross and impurities of your message by tossing the unrelated information.

By grouping and categorizing your existing knowledge, you can identify and list chapter titles and even main supporting points. The result will be a fast and easy writing of your book.

5. *Create framework to house each chapter.*

The best non-fiction books have a set structure to house their chapters. That structure provides the framework for each chapter. It's stressful to re-invent the wheel every time with a blank screen.

Most people including the author are intimidated by a blank screen. Instead of starting from scratch each chapter, use repeating elements to create structure. In John Maxwell's "21 Irrefutable Laws of Leadership: Follow Them and People Will Follow You" foreword by Zig Ziglar contains repeating elements that house each chapter. Each chapter has the same basic form. For example, each of your chapters may contain:

- *Chapter title:* The title immediately followed by a subtitle emphasizes and explains its meaning.

- *Brief quote:* Following the title are one to two quotes from your speeches or other authorities in your field which support the title.

- *Introduction:* Each chapter begins with a six to eight paragraph of introduction that may include a story presenting the chapter's main principle or underlying thesis. For short books 3 to 4 paragraphs sound great.

- *7 to 10 points:* Following the introduction may be lessons or tools used to achieve the goal presented in the introduction. Condense your material as you develop each point. Some lessons may require one paragraph and others may need several.

- *Case studies:* Each chapter may include one or more story form case studies that support the chapter's central idea.

- *Self-evaluation tools:* The chapter may include brief questions that permit readers to measure their progress with each of the principles described in the chapters.

- *Conclusion:* Each chapter may end with four to eight paragraphs that summarize the central idea and supporting points.

- *Other Engagement Tools:* The chapter may include other engagement tools such as worksheets, note sheets, lists that work to engage your readers and make them active participants in the book instead of just observing.

6. *Take easy steps to speed your passionate writing.*

Write your best book now! Have you been guilty of procrastinating on your book project, lately? Like the author, many writers get hung up with wrong thinking about writing and completing their books.

Knowledge and know-how can be formed into nine easy steps that will destroy the power of procrastination. Using the amazingly easy steps below writers can conquer the giant procrastination and speedily write their best book now:

> "Knowledge and know-how can be
> formed into nine easy steps that will destroy
> the power of procrastination."

- *Act Now*. Action will paralyze fear each and every time.
- *Avoid marathon writing*. Know you don't have to become a hermit to write and complete a successful book.
- *Commit to the tracking approach*. Doing a set amount —even if it's only an hour- each day builds a cumulative effect.
- *Know you don't have to write chapters in order*. You can jump around and fill in the blanks to gain momentum.
- *Maintain your momentum*. Don't give in to writers block. Move on to work on the chapter you feel passion bubbling for at that moment.
- *Rewrite & Re-organize*. Be a professional. Don't be lazy and save all the editing for your editor. Make your manuscript the best it can be.
- *Learn to Delegate*. Don't succumb to the idea that you have to do it all yourself if you want it done right. Discern your talents and delegate the rest. Let go faster and profit sooner.
- *Work Efficiently*. Embrace technology. If you don't know how something works, find out. Take a class. Read articles. Learn how to use your software to make things easier and faster.
- *Print Out & Back Up Daily*. Don't believe a computer crash can never happen to you. Save your work somewhere besides your computer hard drive — floppy disk, cd, DVD. Make a hard copy of your manuscript. Print out changes as you work.

Even so, nothing can happen until that first draft is completed. Procrastination is ultimately based on fear of failure. It has stopped countless of book projects and stolen the vision of many more. Don't allow procrastination to become a giant towering over your book dreams.

Step out of your comfort zone prepare your marketing plan, mine your existing knowledge and create a framework for each chapter, speed write your book and you'll be surprised at what you accomplish by following the simple steps of this easy writing program.

7. *Build multiple streams of income.*

The seventh step in making your *Write Your Best Book Now* writing program work includes refining, repeating and repackaging. It involves developing a continuing with a website, a stream of articles, reports and follow-up products and even services to build your brand further.

Once you capture your reader's email addresses and permission to keep in touch with them, you'll want to develop an ongoing stream of articles and even new information products to sell them.

Also, in an ongoing basis you want to review your modules of information and nuggets of information and chunk it into shorter articles, blogs and columns which you will promote with everywhere you can online and in print. Your main goal in submitting articles and columns is not to gain income but opportunities to expose your website URL and book to potential visitors.

Use informational articles and reports. People are online majority of the time looking for free information. Your article can be comprised of a single idea, or a brief overview of the contents you cover in a chapter. Columns interpret more than educate. They permit you to give your opinion on current trends, events or outside influences affecting your readers.

The more exposure you and your website receive the more your credibility builds to support you as an expert and author in your field. Producing your articles for promotion will become easier and easier as you invest time in chunking your knowledge and information.

Email newsletters offer you another opportunity to keep in touch with your readers. Your newsletters can be either informational or opinionated. Either way, they give you an opportunity to remain visible and build even more credibility.

> "The more exposure you and your website receive the more your credibility builds to support you as an expert and author in your field."

Be sure to include your case studies and testimonials to further promote your competent service or product. Technology has advanced making it easier and easier to electronically publish your own e-books. The profits from each sale on a per-unit basis can be 10X the royalties earned by your original book.

The growing possibilities of future income and promotional opportunities are articles, columns, white papers and special reports, journals, workbooks, newsletters (print & online), coaching and consulting.

Though your goal may not be to be a publishing machine -putting out best selling books to formula- but it is important to consider ways to partner with your readers through your website. You can continue to produce articles, books and updates that help you profit from your passion. Each new book or related material will further enhance your visibility and reinforce your credibility as an expert.

SUMMARY

Don't view your book as a one title event. But begin to look at it as the beginning of your successful author journey. If you are looking for an easier journey, more rewards and more profits from your book, follow the principles in the book writing program of the *Write Your Best Book Now* book or its companion 12 week course located at the http://bookwritingcourse.com website. In the following chapters, we'll take a closer look at the new faces of self-publishing.

Chapter 2

THE NEW FACES OF SELF PUBLISHING

The disparaging term "vanity publisher" was actually first used by the publishing industry in the beginning of the 20th century. It was coined to discourage competition. Back then, publishers who used an author's money to print books (an expensive process) could take significant business from the major players in publishing. By implying that 'vanity' publishers were somehow unscrupulous and discrediting the writers as vain, the publishers in business then prevented serious losses.

Let me be clear; self publishing implies that *you* are the *publisher*. In fact, ownership of the ISBN determines who the publisher is. If you didn't buy your ISBNs directly from RR Bowker, you don't own them.

If you do not own the ISBN, you are NOT considered a self publisher in the publishing world. Please remember when I refer to vanity publishers and even POD publishing as self publishing, the term 'self-publishing is loosely used.

Today, there are different kinds of self-publishing, but the term *vanity publisher* still carries weight. <u>In general, it refers to the publisher (sometimes called a book producer) who prints and binds a book in medium to large quantities at the author's sole expense.</u>

The publisher's overhead and profit are included, so vanity publishing is normally more expensive than other kinds of self-publishing. The author owns the completed book and retains all proceeds from sales. It is a known fact, Vanity publishers don't screen for quality. They publish anyone who pays. Some offer additional services such as editing, warehousing, and book fulfillment. They rarely offer marketing or distribution of any kind.

On the other hand, a *subsidy publisher* considered (a joint venture publisher, a co-op publisher, or a partner publisher) also takes payment from the author to print and bind a book. Unlike the vanity publisher, they may contribute a portion of the cost, as well as adjunct services such as editing, distribution, warehousing, and some degree of marketing.

> "Let me be clear; self publishing implies that *you* are the *publisher*. In fact, ownership of the ISBN decides who the publisher is. If you didn't buy your ISBNs directly from RR Bowker or a RR Bowker Authorized Representative, you don't own them. If you do not own the ISBN, you are NOT considered a self publisher in the publishing world.

There may even be some limited screening of submissions to rule out pornography, terrorists or hate literature. Even so, it's not the quality of the author's work that counts. Like with traditional publishers, the completed books become the property of the subsidy publisher, and remain in their possession until sold. The writer receives income from the book through royalty payments.

BOOK PACKAGING is different than subsidy or vanity publishing. Some companies as their business specialize in it. A book packager serves as an independent contractor to produce a predetermined number of your books. All the books belong to you. Book packagers work for a pre-set fee, and all the profits are yours.

When a friend of mine showed off their self-published books at a writers' group meeting, one of the members asked her how she did it. She immediately hired her to produce her book because she didn't want to be bothered with the details. Just like that, she became a book packager! You can do the same with your book(s). The resource section and our new web site make it easy for you to become your own packager and publisher, saving hundreds if not thousands of dollars in the process.

POD PUBLISHING has more to do with the advancement of new technology. Self-publishers who choose this method spend their own money to earn royalties based on sales. Many writers are finding this method most attractive because of the lower upfront cost associated with POD Publishing. As with vanity and subsidy publishing, most POD publishers don't screen manuscripts either. They publish anyone that pays. Some in the publishing world even call the POD publishing option—the new vanity press.

Some POD publishers recommend editors or offer ala carte editing service, but very few insist on editing. Authors may buy as few or as many of their books as they want or can sell. With this method, there are no garages filled with books to worry about. Many writers are finding POD as a useful way to get their book into the market at a relatively low cost and see how well it sells. Most POD publishers offer distribution and often some type of add-on marketing services, but mainly marketing is up to the author.

> "POD is exactly what it says: Print on Demand."

Even now, the term "self-publishing" is most commonly used to discuss publishing that is handled completely by the author. Self-publishing requires the author to undertake the entire cost of publication him/herself. The writer would handle all marketing, distribution, storage, etc.

However, the author can bid out every aspect of the process, rather than accepting a pre-set package of services. Done this way, self-publishing can be more cost-effective than vanity or subsidy publishing. Although it would not be as inexpensive as POD publishing. But unlike POD Publishing and percentage royalty payments, the writer would keep 100% sales proceeds. With a little bit of knowledge, it could result in a higher rate of return as well as a higher-quality product.

WHAT EXACTLY IS POD PUBLISHING?

POD is exactly what it says: *Print on Demand.* This means that books are printed when someone orders them, and they aren't printed unless someone orders them. They aren't stocked (except in minute quantities) in distributor warehouses. Which is for the most part a good thing except when bookstores look them up on their databases they often find that they have to be "backordered?"

POD (Print on Demand) is done on a digital printing press. There are several brands of these machines--Docutech is one; Heidelberg is another. These printers are able to print out a book in a miraculously short period of time (a few minutes), print a cover, bind it and voila, it's ready to go to the shipping department. Print on demand books are usually printed one at a time. They can also be printed in quantities, but these are usually under 500.

> "Unlike offset printing, the POD setup is inexpensive, but the individual cost per book is more costly than offset."

This is a far different from traditional offset printing in which plates had to be made of each page and then printed in large enough quantities to offset the price of the setup. Unlike offset printing, the POD setup is inexpensive, but the individual cost per book is more costly than offset. The way it works, it's usually cheaper to print on an offset press if you're going to print at least 2000 - 3000 or more copies. If you're going to print fewer copies, it's cheaper to do the books on a digital press.

Even so, it doesn't mean that bookstores won't stocks POD books. On the contrary, if the author is personable and the book is good, bookstores often take a chance on local authors. And if the author is smart, then they'll figure out a way to grow that small stock into something larger.

A few years ago Ingram said they wanted to address the "backordering" issue by providing an option to create a "print order" instead. This was supposed to make it easier for bookstores to know how to order these books. Unfortunately, it didn't work that way. At the time of this writing, Ingram has another plan, which POD publishers and authors are anxiously waiting. When it is released, it will make distribution through Ingram a real plus.

SUMMARY

Meanwhile, it's important for you to know how booksellers can order your book through Ingram or through your publisher. With this information, you'll be able to educate the booksellers you contact, and make it easier for you to convince them to carry your book.

Chapter 3

10 MYTHS OF SELF PUBLISHING AND THE TRUTH BEHIND IT ALL

You already have what it takes to self-publish your first book. And like other successful writers you can create or increase your passive income stream each month. Your competitors wish you would never discover the truth about these myths.

You may be asking "What if I don't have what it takes to self-publish?" You do. You've already accomplished the hard part of writing your book. Now it's time to publish it to the world. Believe it or not the world is waiting your unique tips and solutions to their problems in YOUR FIELD. If you want to increase your present income or just get started now, read these ten myth busters and apply them:

Myth 1: No one's interested in buying a self published book.

Truth: There are many self-published authors whose works have sold millions of copies and are still selling because, despite what the major publishing companies say, people want to read what they have to say. Among the most famous self-published authors are:

o   John Grisham: A Time to Kill

o   Walt Whitman: Leaves of Grass

o   Mark Twain: Huckleberry Finn

- o Richard Bolles: What Color is Your Parachute?

- o L. Ron Hubbard: Dianetics

- o Irma Rombauer: The Joy of Cooking

- o Richard Nixon: Real Peace

- o James Redfield: The Celestine Prophecy

And many, many more.

Myth 2: I must have an agent to publish a book.

Truth: If you're unknown writer and you want a major publisher to look at your book, you'd need an agent. Otherwise you do not.

Myth 3: I can't self-publish because it's too expensive for me.

Truth: Self-publishing used to cost several thousands of dollars and sometimes more. But with print-on-demand technology, the major costs are setup costs.

> "The setup costs usually included are typesetting your book, creating cover art, setting up the POD files, assigning ISBNs, arranging distribution, getting your account set up, and other administrative details. Setup costs for print-on-demand range from as low as $400 for a generic looking book with a plain cover to $2000 for a book that would be difficult to distinguish from one produced by a large publishing house."

Myth 4: It's impossible to get a self published book reviewed.

Truth: Self-published books do get reviews. Some even get reviewed in major magazines and newspapers. However, these are the exception, not the rule. Most POD books get reviewed on radio, in local media, in regional magazines, and on the internet.

Myth 5: My self-published book will become an instant best seller.

Truth: If you're Hilary Clinton maybe. Otherwise, prepare yourself for a lot of work just to become known. Some self published books have sold and do sell like that, they are an exception to the norm. Xlibris reported paying one million in royalties last year, but what they didn't say in their PR was that this was to 8000 plus authors -- about $125 per author on average. The reality is a small percentage of authors will make decent money from their book and the rest will sell very little.

Myth 6: The best book for a newbie to write is a novel.

Truth: Actually, non-fiction is your best route. Informative, how-to books sell well on the Internet. Also, they are overall easier to place in bookstores. The main reason for this; people who need information will buy it from any source as long as it looks reputable. After all, what do they stand to lose--a few dollars?

On the other hand, people looking for entertainment or an emotional experience from a book want to know what they're getting before they begin reading. An unknown author of fiction is an emotional risk. What if you don't deliver? I'm not saying there aren't any risk-takers among the reading public. There are; they're just not as plentiful as new writers might wish.

> "Distribution has to do with the availability of books. POD books are distributed through Ingram and Baker and Taylor when the publisher prints through the Ingram print division (Lightning Source aka LSI). If the publisher is actually a printer, he may not use LSI and in that case he will not be able to offer distribution through Ingram. Most POD publishers do offer this distribution, but there are some who charge extra for it."

> "Does it matter if you have Ingram distribution? I think it does. Without it, making your book available is going to be ever more difficult. It won't be listed on Amazon or with other booksellers unless you make those arrangements yourself. Potential readers won't be able to go into a bookstore and have the clerk find your book on their system. Without distribution, your book is virtually invisible. Not many, if anyone will be able to find it."

Myth 7: The only successful books are those published by big name writers or famous people.

Truth: Again, there are self published books that sell notably well and then were picked up by major publishers and made it even bigger. In general, most books make a small income for the author. As long as the book is good to begin with, the more it's promoted to its target audience, the better it will sell.

Myth 8: There is no distribution offered for POD published books.

Truth: Unlike traditional self-publishing, POD publishing often offers some distribution. Some POD publishers charge extra for this, but in reality, POD books are automatically set up to be distributed through Ingram and Baker & Taylor through LSI (the Ingram print on demand division).

Myth 9: All I have to do is write the book. I don't have anything to do with marketing and sales.

Truth: Consider this; there are over a million books in print. I must tell you if you want yours to stand out and sell, you should be prepared to work. Selling books is a business, and it takes hard work just like any other business.

Myth 10: Traditional publishers wouldn't expect me to market my own book.

Truth: Read what a Senior Editor at Harper Collins said: "I won't even look at a book unless the author is prepared to do a book tour and book signings..." There's no way around it; you must be prepared to be your best salesman—market your book.

Myth 11: Bookstores never stock POD published books.

Truth: Never say never; sometimes they will at a local level when dealing directly with the author. They also stock POD published books if they're returnable through Ingram. Otherwise, they probably won't, at least not at the time of this writing. However, this may change very soon when Ingram gets their new stocking/returnability policy up and running.

Myth 12: POD books can't be returned.

Truth: Most POD books are not returnable. Even so, at the time of this writing more and more POD publishers now offer returnability options in their packaged services.

SUMMARY

You can publish a book faster and easier than ever if you know how. People are daily looking for practical information and knowledge that you have. Don't let your ideas, knowledge and expertise fade away. Put it to work for you in your very own book. Remember, take the tips above and bust any self-publishing myths away that hold you back from your successful book.

Chapter 4

WHY PUBLISH ON DEMAND
AND A FEW REASONS WHY NOT

Once upon a time you could count on one hand the number of book publishers that held the fate of your book's future. Now, with the latest technology, online book publishing services can format, publish and print books quickly and affordably.

These companies can work these miracles because of a printing method called print-on-demand (POD) publishing, where books are printed and shipped as they are ordered. It eliminates the need for the offset presses, large print runs and warehousing costs that traditionally come with publishing methods.

Another aspect that POD book publishing services differ from traditional publishers is the rights you have to give up to have your book published. When published traditionally the book publishers own the completed book. With POD publishing, you retain all of your rights (non-exclusive) to the book. Unlike traditional publishers, you are usually required to give up at least a lion's portion of them.

In addition, because POD publishing uses the latest technology, the finished products are as nice as any traditionally published trade book. Additionally, it gives the author a greater royalty earning capacity and eliminates waste in production.

> "POD book publishers also offer a broad selling base, whether it's through their own online bookstore or through online giants such as Amazon.com, Borders.com, Booksamillion.com and Walmart.com."

POD book publishers also offer a broad selling base, whether it's through their own online bookstore or through online giants such as Amazon.com, Borders.com, Booksamillion.com and Walmart.com. Through the distribution channels that reach over 25,000 retailers, today's POD publishers offer the author the ability to sell to brick-and-mortar stores, libraries and other online merchants.

But uppermost in my mind, the best advantage that comes with using POD book publishing service is the greater chance your book is accepted and published. Although, the POD publishing service companies are getting better and do not accept everything that's submitted to them, the POD business model simply allows for a much broader-base of quality books to be printed.

POD SELF PUBLISHING ADVANTAGES

1. *Low Cost*. Yes. You heard it right. It's cheap (anywhere from $499 to $1999 to get published.) It used to be only two ways to get published: Get your book accepted by a major publisher who would then pay you big money in advances against royalties. Or secondly, you could pay for publishing yourself. Until POD publishing technology came on the scene, this was costly. Now, self-publishing the old way (offset)press in quantities of 3000 - 5000 or more costs anywhere from $7000 to $20000 and up, depending on the specs on your book like (trim size, number of pages, cover stock, paper stock, ink, number of books in the run etc.)

ROYALTIES

Royalties are paid to the author for each book sold. Some publishers pay royalties that look high because they're based on "net profit" (this is what's left over after the publisher takes out his expenses). Since there's a lot of room to hedge when dealing with net, it's probably safer to go with a publisher who pays royalties based on list price (the price that the book is supposed to sell for). Even if it sells for less, you still get the same royalty. And even if the publisher's expenses are high, your royalty doesn't change.

2. Distribution. Unlike traditional self-publishing, POD publishing often offers some distribution. Some POD publishers charge extra for this, but in reality, POD books are automatically set up to be distributed through Ingram and Baker & Taylor through LSI (the Ingram print on demand division). If your publisher is actually a printer, he may charge extra for this distribution, or he may not offer it at all. But there are some publishers who use LSI and still charge extra for this just because they can.

3. Higher Royalties. The royalties are much higher than royalties paid by traditional publishers.

4. Non-exclusive Contracts. Most POD publishers offer non-exclusive contracts. This should mean you can publish your book through more than one company if you want to. Though I don't know of anyone that has actually done this.

5.Author Control. You retain the rights to your book which means you remain in control of your books. You can usually cancel the contract very easily.

6. Quick Publishing Process. The publishing process--the time it takes to process your manuscript and see it in print is usually short--anywhere from 8 weeks to several months as compared to a major publisher who could take a year or more.

7. No Large Inventory. The need to do large print runs (and risk losing a lot of money) is eliminated. Additionally, there's no need to warehouse the books that don't immediately sell. So, you don't end up with a garage or basement full of unsold books.

8. No Middleman. There's no need to get an agent or deal with any kind of middleman. According to which company you choose, you can often speak directly with the publisher.

9. Easy Termination. Some publishers allow you to terminate the agreement between you with no more fuss than is required to send written notice.

POD SELF-PUBLISHING DISADVANTAGES

There's a growing amount of POD companies to choose from. Most will not tell you the disadvantages of publishing through print on demand. To their credit, it's not their job to make you aware of the down sides. It's our job as writers and authors to become educated about any business venture. So, in favor of my fellow authors and writers I've taken the challenge to pin-point some of the disadvantages. The disadvantages of POD are these:

1. Distribution: Yes, I know you just read it on the advantage list above. Like most things, it's relative. When compared to the distribution available through other types of self-publishing, it is non-existent. On the other hand, when POD publisher distribution is compared to the distribution offered by major publishers, it becomes a serious disadvantage. At the time of this writing, the problem is that although POD books are available in some 25,000 bookstores, most of those bookstores will not choose to stock them.

Why? For one thing, POD published books is exactly that: print on demand. If there's little to no demand, there's no reason for the bookseller to stock it. By definition, POD published books are ordered when someone orders one. This also makes it difficult to get your book onto bookstore shelves. Even so, remember it's not impossible, but not easy either.

2. Cost: When compared to traditionally published books printed in large quantities, POD books are expensive. The same 200 page book that's printed for two dollars in quantities of 3000 or more, and 75 cents when printed in quantities of 50,000 costs about $4.00 to print through POD. This means it has to be priced higher than books offered by traditional publishers. This is where the POD publisher has to be careful to not price your book out of the market. For example, similar books to yours are priced at 9.95 and your POD published book is priced at 16.95. Which do you think the customer will most likely buy?

HOW CAN I REDUCE THE PRICE OF MY BOOK?

Some POD publishers don't care about this and charge high prices for the books. The author has to get his royalty, and the publisher has to cover costs and make some profit, so there are only three possible ways to lower the retail cost of the book.

☐*One is to use another printer. Unfortunately, the POD industry is limited in that in order to get Ingram distribution (and that includes Baker & Taylor, Amazon, & Barnes and Noble Online) it's necessary to use Ingram's Lightning Source POD division. Every POD publisher offering such distribution is doing so through Lightning.*

☐*The second method is to reduce the price of the book by reducing the number of pages in the book. This can be done by using a smaller font, filling every page with text, by using a larger book size, or by using design elements that increase the amount of text on a page (smaller chapter headings for example).*

☐*Another way to reduce the retail price is to lower the distributor discount. Since part of this discount will go to the bookseller, it's important to be careful when using this method. Go too far and booksellers may think twice; but keep the price too high and retail customers will look elsewhere. It's worth noting that online booksellers will not care too much about how high the distributor discount is. They have no inventory, no store, and very low cost. Anything they make on a book is good.*

However, if bookstores are part of your marketing plan, keep this balance in mind. It's usually inadvisable to lower the discount unreasonably. I wouldn't recommend going lower than 40-45%.

3. Availability: At the time of this writing, booksellers are still being educated regarding POD and often don't know how to order these books. Ingram in recent years, changed their system so that iPage (the Ingram database) will list POD books as having to be "print ordered." But it didn't work very well in convincing booksellers to stock or even order POD published books. POD books used to come up on the Ingram system as "unavailable" or they came up as needing to be "back-ordered." This used to drive both POD publishers and authors crazy. Many booksellers use systems that don't allow backordering. When Ingram changed its systems in the first quarter of 2005 as promised, the change in availability of POD books has been tremendous.

BOOK PRICING

When compared to books that are printed in large quantities, the price of printing on demand, often one-at-a-time, is expensive. A book that costs $.75 when printed in quantities of 50,000 costs about $4 or $5 when printed on demand. Here is how the prices are calculated for a book that is 5x8, 5.5x8.5 or 6x9:

Number of pages x $.015 = cost of book block.
Add to that $.90 for a paperback cover
Or $6 for a laminated hardcover
Or $7.55 for a dust jacketed hardcover.

In addition, book distributors are used to getting a 55% discount. This means that Ingram or Baker & Taylor would get a $10 POD book for $4.50.

4. Returns: Booksellers remain in a risk free position when ordering books from major publishers. Because, the big publishers commit to unlimited returns, a bookseller can order 50 books and then RETURN them all if they don't sell. Although, this is changing POD publishers haven't been able to compete because as self-publishing companies, they don't usually take returns. This began to change a few years ago when a company called Springboard Logistics took on the risk of returns (for a price) through POD publishers. Some authors to level the playing field took returns themselves, and some publishers are working out terms to take returns.

WHAT'S THE BIG DEAL ABOUT BOOK RETURNS?

In the past, POD published book sales were hindered because of the risk involved in stocking them on retail shelves. Traditional publishing houses offer returns, so if an author's book doesn't sell, the bookstore suffers no loss. Therefore, most booksellers aren't interested in taking the risk on an unknown self-published author who can't provide that kind of insurance (no matter how good the book is)?

From the beginning, the inability to receive returns has been a major stumbling block in the POD publishing arena. Even so, some POD companies have leveled the field by making books returnable through Ingram. When you choose to enroll in one of their programs, you remove the risk and make your book more attractive to booksellers everywhere.

In former years, return ability was also implemented at the distribution level. Ingram would only print a copy or two of books that were not returnable. Now, since they've implemented their virtual stocking program, all POD books (except color books at the time of this writing) show up with 100 books in virtual inventory.

Even thought, the benefits of the return ability program are exciting, but it's still up to the author to market the book. Return ability eliminates a huge stumbling block to POD in bookstores and opens the doors wide to POD publishing. It doesn't guarantee book sales, however.

Though, it doesn't take care of all the hurdle here's what it does do. Return ability makes it possible for print-on-demand books to compete like never before with mainstream publishers. Return ability is a necessary element of success for the POD author and the bookseller if the author is going to promote his books to bookstores.

Other necessary elements of success are a well written and edited book, a powerful cover, a good marketing plan, a helpful publisher, and the determination to do whatever it takes to make your book a success.

SUMMARY

Finally, BEWARE of returnability options that are not set up through Ingram. Booksellers do most of their buying through distributors, which provide positive incentives such as the ability to purchase (and return) many books at a time and save on shipping costs. Think of it this way, book return ability through the publisher isn't really much of a deal to the bookseller if they have to pay high UPS fees to ship the book(s) back if they don't sell.

Chapter 5

14 THINGS TO CONSIDER BEFORE CHOOSING YOUR PUBLISH ON DEMAND COMPANY

Technology has advanced in the publishing world. I love it! I have been greatly helped to realize my publishing dreams. I think it's wonderful that aspiring authors have a greater range of choice. Now you may choose to pursue traditional publishing, quantum leap into self-publishing or even POD publishing. Perhaps some would never have the opportunity to see their work in professional print without the arrival of publish on demand or author publishing service companies.

WHAT IS PRINT-ON-DEMAND OR POD PUBLISHING?

Again, Print-on-demand means exactly what it implies: the company print books as they are ordered. They use modern technology to store and print your book in electronic form, removing the need for a warehouse and large print runs.

POD publishing does not take the place of its proud elder brother "Traditional Publishing." As with anything, there are pros and cons of each method. Here's a couple I found interesting: Pros and Cons of POD Publishing by Frank Marshall and the Traditional Publishing vs. Self-Publishing at Scribendi.

With that said, I won't attempt to convince you whether POD publishing is a good choice for you. There are lots of good reports out there on that subject. Back in 2002 when I chose to self-publish my first book, I compiled a report comparing the top three companies.

It helped me make my decision. I have recently revised that report and included Xlibris. It is still one of my most downloaded free reports. If you have decided to publish POD, here are twelve top things to consider and compare.

1. *How do writers feel about this publishing company?*

   Believe me if writers somehow don't like or have become displeased about a company, they usually voice their opinion in print. Look around before selecting a company and see what its authors are saying about them. Or even what some of the industry journalists and writers are reporting. I have heard over and over again from my colleagues, I wish I had known this about them before I selected that company.

   "POD publishing does not take the place of its proud elder brother *Traditional Publishing*."

2. *An attractive and simple to navigate website?*

   Peruse their company website. Take a look at how their books are handled, shopping cart or online bookstore.

3. *An appealing book cover?*

   Covers sell books! Of course it's not the only selling aspect of your book but it is one of the most important. One shot at a good first impression to capture the interest of your potential reader is all you get.

   Author's Note: *Look at their covers in on-line bookstores – back in 2002 I liked what several companies offered but their existing author book covers looked like crayon drawings. Most companies have since improved but I still* *think it's one of the main points to consider. You are looking for bookstore quality or trade quality.*

4. *No lock contracts?*

   Most Publish-On-Demand or print when ordered companies are not considered publishing houses but publishing service companies. Therefore, you should expect a non-exclusive contract period. Look for contracts that have terms that do not lock the author into a contract for long periods of time.

5. *Low or no publishing fee?*

   If you are like most self-publishers you are budget conscious of the initial setup fee of your book. The basic package of the 4 leading companies I researched average about $500. For my first self-published project, I let the other options determine my decision more since my 3 contenders' basic package was about the same.

6. *ISBN, LCCN and bar code?*

   Look for companies that obtain the ISBN (International Standard Book Number), Library of Congress Control Number (LCCN) and bar code for you and at their expense.

7. *Distribution?*

   The publishing service company should list your books with one of the large wholesalers and at least one online retailer. Make sure they list their books in the leading wholesaler database as a part of the package or at least have an add-on option to list in & distribute through the two leading book wholesalers in the United States: Ingram and Baker & Taylor.

8. *Generous royalty payments?*

   You may be wondering like an author friend of mine

asked, "Shouldn't royalty be the first thing I should ask about?" Not necessarily, the traditional publishing company industry standard is 4-8% quarterly or bi-annually.

The industry average for POD companies is about 15-20% at the time of this writing. Even so, it's good to know when to expect your royalty and how much. Most pay quarterly or monthly.

9. *Book price?*

Check for low printing costs and high production value. Find out if they are pricing their books at a competitive market price. It will probably hurt your sales if your book is priced too high above its competitors.

> "Make sure they list their books in the leading wholesaler database as a part of the package or at least have an add-on option to list in & distribute through the two leading book wholesalers in the United States: Ingram and Baker & Taylor."

10. *Author support?*

Know what kind of support the company you contract with will provide. One on One support, representative assigned, phone support, email support are among the options. Find out so you can know what to expect. Make sure you are comfortable with what they propose to provide if you have any problems in the publishing process.

11. *Proof ready?*

Although most POD companies provide proof way ahead of traditional publishing standard of 1-2 years, it's still good to know. You want to know approximately when your book will be ready for your first edit by you the author. Also, if you are running a tight time-line you will want to know for marketing purposes.

12. Books returnable & discounted to bookstores?

Do you plan to sell many books in the bookstore? Books aren't automatically stocked on the precious shelves of bookstores, you know. You should know upfront, if you publish POD publishing more than likely your books are unreturnable.

AUTHOR'S NOTE: Though this is rapidly changing – there are still lots of companies that still go by this policy in their contract. Why is this important? Bookstores expect full trade discount and anticipate buying books on a returnable basis. This includes museums, gift shops, libraries, schools, etc.

---

13. Author purchase discount?

This is important for your marketing campaign. Yes, you do have to market your book. With any self-publishing project, all marketing is considered your responsibility. Even with the economies of traditional publishers you only get a portion of your publicist attention (may be assigned to 10-100 authors) for about 30-90 days.

14. Book marketing help?

You should know most POD publishers don't offer any marketing help included in their package. Yet again, this is rapidly changing. More and more are beginning to offer limited marketing help and aids in their high-end packages. All are offering marketing aids in the form of add-on packages, articles, pod casts and more.

AUTHOR'S NOTE: Let's assume you are an excited author that just finished your book-your labor of love, decided to self-publish, saved $2500 but feel daunted about all the things you have to learn about self-publishing. There are things you must do like hire a cover designer, book editor, someone to professionally layout your book, hire printer, purchase barcodes & ISBN number, etc. Use the information provided in this book to decide if print-on-demand should be your choice.

SUMMARY

We haven't even gotten to the work of marketing. Why not consider a POD publisher who handles all of those stages and steps for you? You are only left with investing in your book at the lowest price possible to re-sell to your readers at whatever price the market will bear. Now that you have decided to self-publish, compare the Publish on Demand companies listed in this book and choose wisely.

Chapter 6

HOW TO SELF PUBLISH YOUR OWN PROFITABLE BOOK

Anyone who can communicate an idea to another person should be able to get their same message across on a written page. If you are either an expert on some subject, or are interested enough to obtain the information for a project, you have what it takes to go from having an idea, to self-publishing your own material in whatever format it develops into.

There are hundreds of publications filled with ads by people just like yourself, who discovered they could make a lot of money writing and publishing their work.

Looking through opportunity magazines, or other publications that cover the field you are interested in, is a good place to start looking for ideas.

Review all the advertisements in the magazines you have chosen to see what popular topics and subjects are being written about in books, manuals, reports and newsletters.

Then ask yourself if you can come up with a better way, or have equally interesting information you can present from a different angle, or with a different twist that would be of interest to the readers in that market. If the answer is "yes," then you can enter that market and also make some incredible money!

CASH IN ON YOUR OWN CREATIVITY AND EXPERTISE

Be creative in developing your material. Perhaps you are aware of some technique that allows people to accomplish their goals faster in a certain field. Maybe you can think of a better way to cash in on a current fad.

The bottom line is that people are hungry for information and ideas, and you can become the writer or self-publisher of information people want to buy. People are eager to buy information that can help them improve their lives:

1) Financially;

2) Physically; and

3) Emotionally.

If you can fill any of those needs with information that can be put onto a written page, there are millions of people waiting to hand over their cash to get it.

FOCUS ON SUBJECT MATERIAL THAT IS SALABLE

Information for your subject matter can be found in various places. For the best results, start with your field of expertise and turn it into a book, manual, report or newsletter.

Focus on providing your targeted market with simple, understandable, and helpful information. It must overwhelmingly appeal to your customers' wants and desires.

> "People are eager to buy information that can help them improve their lives."

Never forget that this is the age of specialized information. People are completely willing to spend their money for tens of thousands of different forms of information, provided it is useful to them. Your job is to either find a need and fill it, or create the need and supply it.

One of the best ways to get started is to sit down with some paper and write down every subject you have some degree of knowledge about. Your list of subjects doesn't have to be in any particular order. Don't force it.

When ideas for headings no longer come easy, stop and start up again at a later time. When you feel comfortable that you have covered most of the areas you know, start picking out the topics that interest you the most. Then you can start researching more material for your writing projects.

FILL YOUR MATERIAL WITH SELF-INTEREST BENEFITS

One of the first things you need to realize is – your book is a product and therefore a business endeavor. Many new writers fail to understand that if they expect any hope for business survival, let alone success, they must come to realize early on that a big part of their job is to arouse the emotions and desires of their customers. Your product, whether a book, manual, report or newsletter, must be portrayed as being jam-packed with self-interest benefits.

Millions of dollars in failed business ventures are wasted every year simply because entrepreneurs fail to understand that what customers want to hear is not necessarily what they have to say. You should never forget this valuable lesson. It can make you rich!

STIR EMOTIONS AND SELL MORE BOOKS

Emotions are what move people to buy anything. Therefore, the job of your product and advertisement vehicle is to move your prospect to buy. You have to stir enough emotions, not only to cause desire, but the rationalization that provides an excuse based on logic.

Even after a prospect makes a commitment to buy your book, etc, they may think they have acted logically. None of your customers will ever admit that emotions had anything to do with their purchase.

What you must always be aware of however, is that logic probably had little to do with the buyer's decision. That is because human actions are often caused by instincts and compulsions that most buyers are unaware of.

As you write your material for publication in any form, or as you develop an ad or other sales package, always think in terms of how a particular benefit will stir a reader's emotions and desires. Try to understand how your product might be perceived by readers by focusing on your own feelings.

Now that you've mastered the shorter forms of writing, perhaps you're ready to write a book-length work of fiction or non-fiction. If you've developed strong writing skills over the course of your writing for profit career, you will likely be able to master the discipline necessary to write a longer work.

The problems are more likely to lie with getting the book published. It is often easier to write a book today than to see it finally get published. Writers frequently see multiple numbers of rejections when submitting to book publishers. Some persist and do well like Richard Bach who survived more than fifteen rejections before getting "Jonathan Livingston Seagull" published. Many others simply give up.

There are other options, however. Getting a book published by a large New York firm is probably the least likely way to break into book publishing. Many of these houses are owned by large corporations today whose interest lies primarily with publishing blockbusters, books that can sell 50-100,000 copies in hard cover. Since few books by established authors do this, the beginner's chance in this market has virtually disappeared.

> "Human actions are often caused by instincts and compulsions that most buyers are unaware of."

In addition, you need an agent in order to approach a large publisher like Random House or Doubleday. If you try to submit directly, your manuscript will likely lay unread. Some may even give you the courtesy of mailing it back. Still others will send you a postcard essentially saying, "Thanks, but no thanks".

The editorial director of the popular magazine, "Publisher's Weekly", believes that self-publishing is the best alternative for new writers to get a book out there for others to see.

If an author is convinced of the quality of his or her book, and is receiving dozens of rejection letters, this editor suggests publishing the book yourself. Comparatively simple equipment, he says, can be used to turn out a reasonable facsimile of a finished book.

This establishes a writer as serious about one's work and can lead to publishers looking at the author's future manuscripts more closely. It always looks good to say you've been published, even if it is self-published.

Some self-publishing books have gone on to bigger and better things. "Bartlett's Familiar Quotations," a standard reference work now was, originally self-published by the author, as was the writer's bible, "The Elements of Style". They sold well; publishers noticed them and bought the rights to publish them in greater quantity.

If you decide to go ahead with self-publishing your book, you will have to be prepared to make an investment. It isn't cheap to publish, but you can save on costs by doing as much work ahead of the printer as possible.

THREE QUICK NON-WRITER WAYS TO GET A BOOK WRITTEN

If you don't have the writer mentality or have the time to go through the 7 step program outlined in chapter 1, you may want to consider these options:

Q/A SYSTEM

Choose your topic of expertise. Ask yourself what are the 25 most important questions regarding this subject matter. Then ask yourself to come up with approximately four subtopics for each of these main 25 questions (topics). Write two pages per night on each of these subtopics. You will have a 200-page book in just over 12 weeks.

ONE PAGE PER TOPIC SYSTEM

Another easy system to put together a book on your topic is the 'one page per topic. Write down every single idea about your topic that comes to mind. Then write something on each topic—regardless of how short or long. You may end up with short blurbs for some topics and five or six pages for others. After writing about each topic, put the topics into categories that make sense. At the end of the exercise, you should have over 200 pages for your book filled with great ideas.

TRANSCRIBE THE SEMINAR SYSTEM

This method has been most effective for non writers. Let's say you don't like writing but love speaking. If you are already an accomplished seminar speaker and own CDs of your work, great. If not, invite six to eight of your favorite friends together, sit them down in a nice room, serve drinks and deliver a seminar.

Be sure to thoroughly outline your topic and have divided so your presentation becomes bite size "modules." These modules will end up being your chapters after all is finished.

Next find someone to transcribe the tapes for a reasonable price. Where you might ask? Start looking at your local community college or university. Next try the senior citizens centers.

GETTING YOUR BOOK EDITED

For many people, this is the most difficult task. Don't be a perfectionist; it's really not that hard. Make sure when you are writing or compiling your book, turn your editor's voice off. You may only turn it back on when it's time for editing.

Again, the best place to start looking for editors is at your local college or university. Ask for the English or Journalism departments to locate student editors. Then hire someone to edit your book for you.

READY TO GO TO PRINT?

The most cost effective way to get your book printed is to provide the printer with a CAMERA READY copy of your manuscript. (Find out what your printer needs) Desk-top publishing software like MS Word or Corel WordPerfect can often let you type set your own book yourself. Or, if not, you should try and type your book on a computer and furnish a typesetter with a disk. It will make it much easier, quicker and less expensive for the typesetter to actually lay the book out in its eventual published format.

If you don't have access to a computer you could have typewritten pages digitized (scan typewritten documents into a computer.) There's usually a fee for taking your manuscript off a disk and preparing it for book production. This process is referred to as typesetting or layout. Also, don't forget Resource Section at the end of this book for easy Book Design Wizard software to professionally lay your book out.

Next, work with a graphic artist to design the cover. A photograph of you as author will likely suffice for the back cover copy. Also, in the Resource Section you will find a link to Book Cover Pro, a software program to help you design your book cover in style and excellence. Using this software you can produce a cover that competes in the market place.

QUICK LIST OF FACTORS THAT AFFECT YOUR BOOK COST

☐Book dimensions (6"x9", 81/2 x 11", et.c)

☐Type of binding (perfect binding, hard bound, comb-bound, saddle stitched, velo-bound, wire-o-bound) see glossary for terms.

☐Kind of paper used for cover

☐Number of ink colors on cover and in text.

☐Number of pages in text (include title page, table of contents, index, each and every page)

☐Quantity of books desired.

☐How prepared your manuscript is.

Print your book in soft cover. It's cheaper to print and thus you can keep your book priced lower for resale. This could improve the volume of your actual sales. The most popular book size is 5 x 8 inches. Depending on typeset size, there are usually 350-400 words per page. It is easy to fit this book on your shelf, in a briefcase, or in an overnight bag for airplane reading, thus making it a good size to market. Many original soft cover paperbacks are in this standard size.

Have the book perfect-bound on 60 pound offset paper. The text printing should be black. The cover should be in 2 colors while the cover stock should be 10 point coated, one side only.

Look for a printer who can print a book. Few can do this effectively; no matter what they say they can do! Get at least three or four price quotes. The unit cost of each book will vary depending on the volume of copies you print. 5,000 books, for example, will have a much smaller per book cost than will printing of the 500 books. Or don't forget to consider sites like booksjustbooks.com or instantpublisher.com They are essentially Internet book printers but they offer affordable options to get your book printed.

> "Desk-top publishing software can often
> let you type set your book yourself."

The reason is due to the high cost of setting the machine to print. Once the press is running, you simply pay for the paper and materials. Don't have 5,000 books printed, however, simply to save on your unit cost. If you don't anticipate selling that many books, start with ordering just a few.

Judge how many you think you can sell and then have that number printed. You can always do a second printing cheaper than the first, since the set-up charges will not repeat unless you make changes to the book.

What price do you set for the book? Much depends on the market and your own costs in printing the book. Go down to your local bookstore and see what the range of prices are on books of your size and style (soft cover). If the average price is $12.95, this will tell you what a competitive charge would be.

Now, contrast that with the unit cost of your book which is the total printing, typesetting and graphic arts charges for your books divided by the number of copies. If your unit cost is, say, $3.50 per book, you'd like to ideally charge about three or four times the cost on the open market, which would be around $10.50 to $14.00, for which the $12.95 average price fits quite nicely.

SUMMARY

Now that you understand the options or being your own publisher, you are only left with investing in your book at the lowest price possible to re-sell to your readers at whatever price the market will bear. Now that you have decided to self-publish, compare the options and choose wisely.

Chapter 7

TWO OTHER FACES OF SELF PUBLISHING

A re you willing to discover another face of self-publishing in the new millennium. I couldn't write this book without including what I consider my best kept secrets. I know these options are not for every one. But it's worth letting you choose.

The two other options to consider if you're thinking about self-publishing your book: You can consider compiling your book as an ebook yourself and selling it from your own web site. Also, you can set up a publishing company and print your book using the same company most of the print-on-demand service companies use to print their authors' books. In short, you can become your very own independent publisher. As an *indie publisher,* you can publish your own work and the work of others.

Choosing either of these options, you may need some additional software or technology to make your books and ebooks look professional. Or you can do what you're best at (writing the book) and sub-contract the rest to a skilled professional(s).

Self-publishing truly is a great way to try out new book ideas and bring them to market faster than going through traditional publishing. A traditionally published book could take six to eighteen-months before its released. If your information is time-sensitive, it could be obsolete by the time it goes to print.

Then there's the well known fact that traditional publishers pay only a small percentage to the author - around 6%-10%. Self-publishing offers larger profit margins. Even so, the main benefit in going with a traditional publisher is that they release your book out to a larger audience through their national and international distribution channels. They have the Big Company name brand muscle to catapult your book to new levels.

They also may hire a publicist to help you get press coverage. But, you'll still have the main responsibility of your own marketing. If your book doesn't sell well within the first 90 days, they may take their losses and spend no additional time or money on promoting it.

If you decide to self-publish, first decide the main format of your book. I suggest getting your print book done first then release your book in ebook format (including some of the other formats listed later in this book) from your web site.

PRINT BOOKS

STEP ONE: When creating a printed book using this print on demand option, you eliminate the middlemen called author service companies. You are your own publisher. You may create a publishing company or start a publishing division of a company you currently own. As publisher, your first step is to obtain a block of ISBN's. ISBN numbers are sold in 10-packs for around $245. You can purchase them from http://www.isbn.org . After you assign an ISBN to a book, you need to list it in their online database.

What You Should Know - about ISBN Numbers & Bar Codes!

What is an International Standard Book Number (ISBN)? The International Standard Book Number (ISBN) is a number that uniquely identifies books and book-like products published internationally.

The purpose of the ISBN is to establish and identify one title or edition of a title from one specific publisher. The ISBN is unique to that edition, allowing for more efficient marketing of products by booksellers, libraries, universities, wholesalers, and distributors.

If you have established your own publishing company-basically, a name and an address to begin with-you can purchase ISBNs from R.R. Bowker, the U.S. agency licensed to sell them. They cost $225 plus a small handling fee for a minimum of ten numbers. The usual turnaround time is ten business days for non-priority processing. For an additional fee, your application can be processed in three business days.

If you are producing both paperback and hardback versions of your book, you will need two different ISBN numbers to identify them. To get all the details directly from R.R. Bowker, including the required forms, go to the self-publishing tab and click "Obtaining an ISBN" from the list of resources.

Do I really need my own ISBN? Yes. The ISBN is what identifies you as the publisher. Once you have obtained your ISBNs from R.R. Bowker, you are no longer a "self publisher." You are considered a "publisher" . . . an independent publisher. There's no difference at that point between you and Harper Collins except for the fact that Harper Collins publishes more titles than you (more than most publishers, for that matter).

As publisher, you assign one of these numbers to your first book. After you own the ISBN, it remains the same for the life of the book. You can change printers, distributors, wholesalers, retailers, or whatever else you want-the book remains yours. It's important to note that if, ten years from now, someone orders a copy of your book, you, as the publisher, will get the order. If you don't own the number, the person who does will get the order.

May I have someone assign me one of their ISBNs? No. The most popular option offered by today's vanity/subsidy presses is to tell you that they will "assign" or "sell" you an ISBN. They lead you to believe that your book is registered in your name and reinforce this by telling you "You retain all the rights." This is all a play on wording.

No one can give or assign you a number. They can let you use one of their numbers, but you do not own it. The orders for that book (ISBN) will always go to that publisher. If you change publishers, the ISBN does not go with you; it remains theirs. You will need to start all over with your marketing efforts under your new ISBN number.

Even worse than the vanity presses are a new group of companies that present themselves as resellers of single ISBNs. Remember: There are no companies in the United States that can sell you a legitimate ISBN identifying you as the publisher except R.R. Bowker. Anyone who tells you different is not telling you the whole truth.

WHAT ABOUT BAR CODES?

Your book ISBN is translated into a internationally compatible bar code format called a Bookland EAN (European Article Number). Every bookstore chain and most smaller bookshops use bar code scanning at the checkout register.

Your book cover designer can easily put the bar code on your book. Using a software program, the designer types in your ISBN, and the bar code comes up in just the right place on your back cover.

After you apply for your ISBN's, they'll give you a username and password for their site where you can add your book(s) to their database. The good news about this method of self-publishing is when your book is added, it will automatically be listed in Books In Print catalog that bookstores use to order books.

At the time of this writing, some of the author service companies don't tell you this and charge an additional fee to list you in the Books In Print catalog. Being listed in the Books In Print catalog means, if someone goes into a bookstore and asks for your book, the average bookseller can look it up and order it.

STEP TWO: The next step is finding your printer. Traditionally, you would have to do a print run of several thousand copies which would cost thousands of dollars, but today, with print on demand, creating a paperback book is faster and cheaper than ever. You can print one, ten, twenty or hundreds of books quickly and without tying up all your money in inventory that may or may not sell.

The best place for this print-on-demand option is http://lightningsource.com. They are known for their high quality work. On top of that it's delivered quickly and economically. They produce paperback, hardback or electronic books (ebooks) for you. You send them your book manuscript and cover in the appropriate Adobe PDF format and a proof will be in your hand in about a week!

For a printed book, I recommend hiring a professional artist to do your cover and instruct them to deliver it to you in PDF format so you can send it directly to Lightning Source. A good book cover design will usually cost you from $100-$300 - possibly more if you must pay a photographer for reprint rights on any artwork.

Or here's another good software resource to consider if you are starting on a shoe-string budget or plan to release several books: http://BookCoverPro.com The templates and the software will help your design a book cover yourself to equal that of a professional. It even has a pdf converter function that will convert your cover into the format readily accepted by Lightingsource.com, Lulu.com and BookSource.com.

I recommend Adobe InDesign or PageMaker to layout your books and create the PDF's that Lightning Source needs. Also, a good alternative would be Book Design Wizard software located at http://www.self-pub.net/. You just input your finished book into this software and it handles the margins and layout of your book.

Additionally, to make sure you send your manuscript in the format they accept visit LightningSource.com book designer resource section for instructions and templates. With Lightning Source you can set your book up in their system for about $100 and from there you may print as few or as many books as you'd like.

Just to give you an idea, a paperback 8.5x5.5 with a full color cover and approximately 224 pages inside will run you around $4.35 to produce.

Now you may be thinking, I could produce the same book for around $2.00 if I used a traditional publisher (vanity publisher) like Morris Publishing, but you'd have to have a thousand or more printed at once.

You can submit digital files of your book to Lightning Source and literally have a stack of books delivered to your door within two weeks. Orders after the initial setup take only about a week to receive. If you're on a shoe-string budget, in a hurry to market, or you just want to see how sales go before you invest thousands of dollars, consider print on demand.

ABOUT DISTRIBUTION

STEP THREE: The biggest hurdle for most self-publishers is getting their books in bookstores. Did you know most major publishers actually buy shelf space in bookstores? So the little guys have little or no possibility of receiving shelf space in a traditional bookstore - much less prominent placement.

But it is possible to obtain virtual shelf space on Amazon, Wal-Mart, Barnes & Noble and BooksAMillion's Web sites. Another great thing about Lightning Source is that they are a subsidiary of Ingram Book Sellers and your book is automatically distributed by Ingram and Baker & Taylor.

This means that after your book is created with Lightning Source, it's automatically listed on Amazon, Wal-Mart, BarnesandNoble.com and BooksAMillion.com! Another option, some author service companies charge extra for.

With targeted marketing, you can also get shelf-space in smaller bookstores because almost everyone purchases from Ingram or Baker & Taylor. In the Christian market, Spring Arbor is the major distributor and since they are a subsidiary of Ingram, approved Christian titles will also be distributed by Spring Arbor.

This means anytime Amazon (any other Internet) or brick and mortar bookstore sells your book, they purchase from the distributor (Ingram, Baker & Taylor or Spring Arbor) at the wholesale price. The distributor fills the order and cuts you a check approximately three months later based on your total sales for the month.

You don't have to touch the books or tie up any money. Everything is handled between the Distributor and the Bookseller. Your main challenge is waiting for your check to arrive.

PUBLISHING TIP: Did you know that you could actually get on the New York Times Best Seller List without your book being in brick and mortar bookstores? Get enough publicity - radio, print and TV promotion - and send people to Amazon or Barnes and Noble Online and those sales will count toward the New York Times Best Seller list! Once you've hit that, you know every bookstore in America will want your book on their shelf - self-published or not!

ELECTRONIC BOOKS (eBooks)

Publishing electronic versions of your book has several benefits which include:

- You can cash in on the renewed interest in ebooks via Amazon Kindle, Apple's iPad, Barnes & Noble's Nook and a host of other PDA's.

- They have very little cost associated with them. Thousands are as simple to sell as one.

- Fulfillment is instantaneous and doesn't require labor on your part.

- There are no shipping costs.

- You can literally make money while you sleep!

The downsides to ebooks may include:

- Not everyone is willing to read a book online or print it

themselves, so you could miss out on sales by limiting yourself to only an electronic version.

- There are several ebook formats, and you may need to learn to produce versions in Kindle's .MOBI, iPad's and BN's .ePub, Adobe, Palm Pilot and for other PDA's.

EBOOK CREATION

Assuming you have written your book, the next step is easy. You save it into an electronic format(s) which can be read by others. If you only want to sell your ebook on your personal website, most desktop computer users choose Adobe Reader. But if you want to take advantage of the renewed interest via eReaders, Kindle, iPad & the Nook then you need to convert your book into respective formats .mobi and .epub. Microsoft Reader is common for PDA's and many people have Palm Pilots.

Adobe Format

You'll need the Adobe Writer software to create an Adobe PDF file that can be read by Adobe Reader. At the time of this writing, this software normally costs about $200-300.

SHOE-STRING BUDGET TIP: At the time of this writing, You can go to the http://www.adobe.com site and click the link for Create Adobe PDF Online. They'll let you create 5 Adobe files for free and then they have a service available where you can pay $9.99/MONTH TO CREATE AS MANY AS YOU Want. Or visit the resource section at the end of this book and find out where to go get free software and sites to create PDFs.

If you plan to create more than one printed book or need more versatile desktop publishing features, consider purchasing Adobe InDesign or Adobe PageMaker and the Acrobat Writer comes with it.

It's recommended to convert your ebook(s) to other versions / formats to cater to the rising popularity of various ebook readers. You can either do it yourself through Calibre http://calibre-ebook.com/ which is an excellent all-in-one ebook management software or just submit your free ebooks to great sites out there that auto-convert your ebooks to various other formats. Some of them include:

a. *Smashwords - http://www.smashwords.com/*
b. *Manybooks - http://manybooks.net/*
c. *Feedbooks - http://www.feedbooks.com/*

The two most popular e-book formats used in eReaders are the Mobi Format, commonly known as the Kindle format, and the .ePub, known to be the native format for Stanza. ePub is the Open eBook standard from the International Digital Publishing Forum (http://www.idpf.org/). ePub is supported in Stanza Desktop, iPhone, and iPod Touch, as well as in Adobe Digital Editions, Apple's iBooks, and the next generation of e-ink readers like the Sony Reader (PRS-505).

Although both are popular formats, you should look at the whole picture before making your decision. As always, there are pros and cons of using either format. I am a do-it-yourselfer and an educator; so I love trying new techno gadgets. I usually report to my readers and students my findings.

I purchased my Kindle first and the iPad later; I developed all my ebooks for the Kindle platform using the .mobi format. Plus, at the time of this writing Amazon offers 70% to its ebook authors and publishers.

As my schedule permits I will convert them to the .epub format to gain greater exposure.

1. Mobipocket/Kindle

Overview: Mobipocket, a French company that began in the days when Palm Pilots and other PDAs were front and center. It's said the company developed their reading software and ebook creation when eBooks were still in their infant stages. They managed to thrive in the infant market. They were eventually purchased by Amazon giant in 2005. When Amazon first developed the Kindle, the company used their own proprietary format for their ereader's eBooks.

- *Amazon Kindle*
- *Format: Kindle*
- *Published as: .azw*

With the launch of the Kindle eBook reader, Amazon.com created the proprietary format, AZW. It is based on the Mobipocket standard, with a slightly different serial number scheme (it uses an asterisk instead of a dollar sign) and its own DRM formatting. Because the eBooks bought on the Kindle are delivered over its wireless system called Whispernet, the user does not see the AZW files during the download process. The Kindle format is now available on a variety of platforms.

In 2008, Oprah announced the Kindle as one of her favorite things. The Kindle catupultaed to front and center stage. The Mobipocket format is based loosely on HTML 3.2 and includes some unique formatting requirements. In recent years, development on the display engine and HTML support appears to have stagnated, but the number of users using the format kept growing, especially with the Kindle becoming so popular.

Devices: Mobipocket books can be read in Mobipocket Reader on Windows PCs, Blackberrys, Symbian smartphones, and Windows-based smartphones, as well as natively on the Kindle and a few other eBook devices.

Extensions: Mobipocket/Kindle files come in three different file extensions: .mobi, .prc, and .azw. There are no functional differences between these formats, and the files themselves are exactly the same.

2. ePub/ IDPF/ EPUB

Overview: The ePub format has developed as an industry-wide standard for eBooks. It is based on a variety of other technologies and standards, like Open eBook and XHTML 1.1.

Its uniqueness is in how it combines these standards to provide a solid formatting foundation for eBooks of just about every shape and size. The display engines for ePub books have not quite caught up with the formatting standards. Even so, the formatting possibilities in ePub books have moved beyond all the other formats.

DRM: The most popular DRM option for ePub files is Adobe Content Server, which is utilized by Sony, Barnes & Noble, and many other eBook stores. Apple's iBooks appplication (on the iPad) utilizes Apple's own Fairplay DRM, which is not compatible with any other eBook device or application.

The ePub standard is maintained by the International Digital Publishing Forum (IDPF), a non-profit organization made up of technology and publishing companies.

The EPUB logo and format (.epub) or OEBPS format is an open standard for e-books created by the International Digital Publishing Forum (IDPF). It combines three IDPF open standards: Open Publication Structure (OPS) 2.0, which describes the content markup (either XHTML or Daisy DTBook); Open Packaging Format (OPF) 2.0, which describes the structure of an .epub in XML. and OEBPS Container Format (OCF) 1.0, which bundles files together (as a renamed ZIP file)

Devices: Currently, the format can be read by the Kobo eReader, Apple iBooks, Barnes and Noble Nook, Sony Reader, BeBook, Bookeen Cybook Gen3 (with firmware v. 2 and up),COOL-ER, Adobe Digital Editions, Lexcycle Stanza, BookGlutton, AZARDI, Aldiko and WordPlayer on Android and the Mozilla Firefox add-on EPUBReader. Several other reader software programs are currently implementing support for the format, such as dotReader, FBReader, Mobipocket, uBook and Okular. Another software .epub reader, Lucidor, is in beta.

Adobe Digital Edition uses .epub format for its e-books, with DRM protection provided through their proprietary ADEPT mechanism. The recently developed INEPT framework and scripts have been reverse-engineered to circumvent this DRM system. DSLibris, a Sourceforge.net project, is able to decode e-books in .epub and .xht format for reading on Nintendo DS systems.

3. Microsoft Reader

Many PDA's read Microsoft Reader. The software for creating Microsoft Reader files merges itself into your Microsoft Word program and looks like a little green and brown tree button on your menu bar. You may download at
http://www.microsoft.com/reader/downloads/pc.asp
Additionally, the free download is also available for Pocket PCs:http://www.microsoft.com/reader/downloads/ppc.asp When you are ready to create your ebook in Microsoft Word, then click the little tree icon that MS Reader puts on your Microsoft Word Toolbar and follow the prompts from there.

4. Palm Pilot

Lots of people use palm pilot, so you shouldn't leave them out. To create a file that can be read on a Palm Pilot, you'll need your book stored in a text file with special markup codes for bolding, underlining, centering and italicization. You can view your books in Palm Reader format on your desktop computer.

To create the Palm Reader document, you'll need a program like DropBook which is available as a free download located at the website: http://www.palmdigitalmedia.com/dropbook .

You don't need a Palm Pilot to view your books in Palm Reader format on your desktop computer. You just need their software for your desktop, which is available for free http://www.palmdigitalmedia.com/products/palmreader/trial

DELIVERY

It's always good to provide your customers with options. So you can use Paypal and/or Clickbank to sell and deliver your ebook. the process is simple; if you know what to do. And here's what you do, you store your ebook on your Web site and then set the

Paypal and/or Clickbank "thank you" page to automatically take the customer to a Web page on your site where they can download your ebook in their format of choice.

Make sure you give them links for where they can download the Adobe Reader, Apple's iPad, BN's Nook, Amazon Kindle, Microsoft Reader or Palm Pilot software. If you manually process orders, you can always have a standard email you send to people once their order is processed that tells them where to go to download the ebook or have the ebook attached.

It's best to set it up where your ebook is delivered automatically and your system redirects your customer to the thank you page. With all the spam emails floating around, your standard email with an attachment may not make it to your customer creating unnecessary customer service calls.

SUMMARY

Don't let the title *Publisher* make you afraid. You can do it. You can self-publish your own book in style and excellence. Now go to your destiny. <u>Make it different, make it count, make it YOUR</u> self-published book. Your audience is waiting on your important message to change their life.

Chapter 8

15 SIMPLE COPYRIGHT TIPS YOU NEED TO KNOW

Copyright simply means *the right to copy* and <u>plagiarism</u> means *copied word for word*. The law gives you copyright protection automatically upon the creation of your work. Your work does not have to be completed to be protected. You own the copyright on your work as you create it. No publication or registration or other action in the U.S. Copyright Office is required to gain copyright.

After you gain the knowledge about basic copyrighting what you can and should not do, allow your conscience to be your guide. If you are knowledgeable about basic copyrighting and you feel doubtful about it get permission. Follow these 15 tips about basic copyrighting and respect another's writer's work as you want yours to be respected.

1. *In general, copyright registration is voluntary.* Copyright protection exists from the moment the work is created (fixed in tangible form). Even so, you will have to register, if you wish to bring a lawsuit for infringement of a U.S. work.

2. *Registration of your work is recommended* even though copyright protection is automatic because:

> "Copyright protection exists from the moment the work is created (fixed in tangible form)."

d. Registration establishes a public record of the copyright Claim,

e. issues a certificate of registration,

f. Before an infringement suit may be filed in court, registration is necessary for works of U.S. origin. Additionally, may be eligible for statutory damages $500 - $20,000 (as determined by the judge) and attorney's fees in successful litigation. If the plaintiff proves that the defendant's infringement was "committed willfully," the judge may award damages as high as $100,000 per infringement. 17 U.S.C 504(c).

g. Additionally, if registration occurs within five years of publication, it is considered prima facie (adequate to establish a fact unless refuted) evidence in a court of law.

h. Registration allows the owner of the copyright to record the registration with the U.S. Customs Service for protection against the importation of infringing copies.

3. *Publication is not necessary for copyright protection.* It used to be but is no longer required.

4. *How do I find the copyright symbol on my computer?* Every good word processor today gives you access to important characters that do not appear on the keyboard. They are called ANSI and ASCII character sets. To get the © character, make sure the Num Lock key on the right-hand side of your keyboard is on, and use those numbers for coding the character (the numbers at the top of the keyboard will not work). Now, hold down the Alt

key and press 0169. When you release the Alt key, © will appear where your cursor is.

5. *To register a work,* you need to submit a completed application form, a non-refundable filing fee of $30, and a non-returnable copy or copies of the work to be registered.

6. *The registration process length* normally depends on the amount of material the Office is receiving. If your application is in order, you may generally expect to receive a certificate of registration within approx. 4-5 months of submission.

7. *Using someone else's work without getting permission*
   Under the fair use doctrine of the U.S. copyright statute, it is permissible to use limited portions of a work including quotes, for purposes such as commentary, criticism, news reporting, and scholarly reports. There are no legal rules permitting the use of specific number of words, a certain number of musical notes, or percentages of work. Whether a particular use qualifies as fair use depends on all the circumstances.

8. *In the case of "work made for hire", the employer or commissioning party is considered to be the author?* Under the copyright law, the creator of the original expression in a work is its author. The author is also the owner of the copyright unless there is a written agreement by which the author assigns the copyright to another person or entity, such as a publisher. In cases of works made for hire, the employer or commissioning party is considered to be the author.

"To register a work, you need to submit a completed application form, a non-refundable filing fee of $30, and a non-returnable copy or copies of the work to be registered."

9. *Copyright does not protect names, titles, slogans, or short*

phrases. Nor does it protect ideas, concepts, systems, or methods of doing something, only expressions of creative effort.

10. *The (c) has no legal force as of yet.* It must be the word "copyright" or the official copyright symbol ©.

11. *Publishing on the internet* is not automatically public domain.

12. *Copyright law is mostly civil law.* However, new laws are moving copyright violation toward the criminal arena.

13. *The copyright generally last* until 70 years after the author dies. (see the Copyright Office's FAQ for details)

14. *A list of commonly requested forms* arranged by the type of copyrighted work:
    a. Books, manuscripts and speeches and other non-dramatic literary works: *Form TX*
    b. Computer programs: *Form TX*
    c. Music sheets or lyrics: *Form PA*
    d. Music sound recordings: *Form SR*
    e. Cartoons and comic strips: *Form VA*
    f. Photographs: *Form VA*
    g. Drawings, prints, and other works of visual arts: *Form VA*
    h. Motion pictures and video recordings: *Form PA*
    i. Dramatic Scripts, plays, and screenplays: *Form PA*
    j. Games: *Form TX*

15. *A mandatory deposit is a requirement of the Copyright Office* that copies of all works under copyright protection that have been published in the U.S. have to be deposited with their office within three months of the date of publication.

16. A work in *public domain* is one that can be freely used by anyone for any purpose. In the past, if a work was published without notice, it lost all copyrights and

entered the public domain. This is no longer true. There are still some instances a work is considered public domain: copyright expired, U.S. government work, category that can't be copyrighted (i.e. names, titles, short phrases, etc.)

I strongly encourage you to copyright your self-published material and it is recommended that you also register your book and obtain an International Standard Book Number (ISBN). To do this, you must write to a couple of organizations. First up is the Copyrights Office. You should write to:

Register of Copyrights
Copyrights Office
Library of Congress
Washington, DC 20599

Ask for the copyright registration forms and the booklet entitled "Copyright Basics". This will give you explicit instructions on copyrighting your material. Copyright protection now lasts for your lifetime plus fifty years.

FACTS ABOUT COPYRIGHTS

Copyright is a widely misunderstood concept. The fact is, everything you've ever written, from your school notes to family bulletins, is yours, and unless you copied it from a copyrighted source, you own the copyright. This simple legal principle is accepted in most free-world countries, but it's almost useless to you in a court of law without some sort of proof.

The simplest way to assert copyright is to print (C) Your Name, Year. You'll notice we use this notification on much of our material. It is not necessary to add the legal warning which we use, however.

You can protect your copyright cheaply, and with a high degree of legal protection, by sealing the item to be copyrighted in a tamper-proof envelope, stamping the envelope over any point where the envelope could be opened, having your postal clerk postmark the stamps over the seal points, and mailing it back to yourself.

Label the envelope for future reference, and if you can, smudge the fresh postmark ink so there's a gray blotch between stamp and envelope. It can be scrutinized in court for tampering, and any half-decent forensic scientist will be able to shoot down any zealous attorney who tries to prove you faked it. You can copyright whole books this way for under $2.00.

You are not strictly required to register your copyright, but it is the best protection, and again if you do wish to copyright, write to:

The Registrar, CIP Division
Library of Congress
Washington, DC 20540

It costs money to register a copyright, so unless you really require solid protection, or demand confidentiality, it may not be worth your while.

You can put your book's retail price near the bar code on the back cover if you want to.

Even so, that doesn't mean that retailers will always have to charge the full amount. Using their computers, they can connect your Bookland EAN code to a sale price, and that's the price that will appear on the register when your book is purchased and scanned.

If you are using a bar code, it must be black or a color dark enough to be scanned. Keep this in mind when counting the number of colors on your cover. Additionally, please know it's not necessary to buy bar codes from R.R. Bowker when you buy your ISBNs. Your cover designer should have the software needed to generate a bar code. At the time of this writing, where ever you buy the bar code, you don't have to pay more than $25 for it.

While we're on the subject of copyrighting, you can also obtain a Library of Congress catalog card and number for your book. It is free to do so, at the time of this writing. Libraries around the country often use this number to identify books and order them.

As I have said earlier, the International Standard Book

Number (ISBN) is another type of classification system for a book. Libraries, bookstores and wholesalers all use this number system for ordering books.

As a self-publisher, you will be assigned a number prefix which is part of the ISBN. Thereafter, for future publications, you will assign your own ISBN based on the pre-assigned codes you'll receive. To get more information about this, write to:

ISBN Agency

R.R. Bowker & Company

205 E. 42nd Street

New York, NY 10017

Ask specifically for the "ISBN System User's Manual" and the "ISBN Log Book" when contacting the ISBN Agency.

SUMMARY

All of this work, including copyrighting, ISBNs and Library of Congress cataloguing is crucial in establishing your book as a professional entry. You have a far better chance of having your work noticed by your readers and professionals in the industry if it is officially filed.

Just because it's a self-published work doesn't mean it isn't a good book and worthy of attention. Establishing your work in this way enhances your image and your potential as a serious writer.

Publishing yourself can be a rewarding experience and can launch a whole new career for you. If you like to write, book publishing can be a worthy goal.

Chapter 9

21 FREQUENTLY ASKED COPYRIGHT QUESTIONS ANSWERED

1. Who is an author?

Under copyright law, the creator of the original expression in a work is its author. The author is also the owner of copyright unless there is a written agreement by which the author assigns the copyright to another person or entity, such as a publisher. In cases of works made for hire, the employer or commissioning party is considered to be the author.

2. Do I have to be published to obtain copyright?

No, Publication is no longer the key to obtaining federal copyright as it was under the Copyright Act of 1909. The 1976 Copyright Act defines publication as follows:

"Publication" is the distribution of copies or phono-records of a work to the public by sale or other transfer of ownership, or by rental, lease, or lending. The offering to distribute copies to a group of persons for purposes of further distribution, public performance, or public display constitutes publication. A public performance or display of a work does not of itself constitute publication.

3. If Publication is not required why is it important to the Copyright law?

Before 1978, federal copyright was generally secured by the act of publication with notice of copyright, assuming compliance with all other relevant statutory conditions...Publication is an important concept in the copyright law for several reasons:

- Works that are published in the U.S. are subject to mandatory deposit with the Library of Congress.

- Publication of a work can affect the limitations on the exclusive rights of the copyright owner that are set forth in sections 107-121 of the law.

o The year of publication may determine the duration of copyright protection for anonymous and pseudonymous works (when the author's identity is not revealed in the records of the Copyright Office) and for works made for hire.

o Deposit requirements for registration of published works differ from those for registration of unpublished works. *See Registration Procedures.*

o When a work is published, it may bear a notice of copyright to identify the year of publication and the name of the copyright owner and to inform the public that the work is protected by copyright. Copies of works published before March 1, 1989, must bear the notice or risk loss of copyright protection.

4. *Is acknowledging the source of the copyrighted material substitute for obtaining permission?*

No, it does not.

5. *How do I get permission to use somebody else's work?*

You ask for it. If you know who the copyright owner is, you may contact the owner directly. If you are not certain about the ownership, you may request the Copyright Office to do a search of its records for $75 per hour.

6. *Can I be sued for using someone else's work, like quotes or samples?*

If you use a copyrighted work without authorization, the owner may be entitled to bring an infringement action against you. There are some circumstances under the "fair use" doctrine where a quote or a sample may be used without permission.

7. *What is a Library of Congress number?*

The Library of Congress Card Catalog Number is assigned by the Library at its discretion to assist librarians in acquiring and cataloging works.

8. *What is an ISBN number?*

The International Standard Book Number is administered by the R.R. Bowker Company 1-888-BOWKER2. The ISBN is a numerical identifier intended to assist the international community in identifying and ordering certain publications.

9. *What is the copyright notice?*

A copyright notice is an identifier placed on copies of the work to inform the world of copyright ownership. It was once required, is now is optional. The identifier is © the C inside a circle and the word copyright. The c in parenthesis has no legal recognition at this time.

10. *Someone infringed on my copyright. What can I do?*

A person may seek to protect his or her copyrights against unauthorized use by filing a civil lawsuit in the Federal district court. *The Copyright Office's advice is: If you believe that your copyright has been infringed, consult an attorney. They inform that in cases of willful infringement for profit, the U.S. Attorney may initiate a criminal investigation.*

11. *Is my copyright good in other countries?*

The U.S. has copyright relations with more than 100 countries throughout the world, and as a result of these agreements, we honor each other's citizens' copyrights. However we don't have these agreements with every country.

12. What does the Copyright Office mean when they posted "Our mail has been severely disrupted?"

For security reasons, all U.S. Postal Service and private carrier mail is being screened off-site prior to arrival at the Copyright Office. Please be aware that this screening process can add 3-5 days to the delivery time for all mail to the Copyright Office.

13. About "All Rights Reserved"

All rights reserved is considered another formality of the U.S. publishing community. It gains its roots from one of the earliest international copyright treaties in which the U.S. was a member, the 1911 Buenos Aires Convention on Literary and Artistic Copyrights. This treaty provided that, once copyright was obtained for a work in one signatory country, all other signatories accorded protection as well without requiring any further formalities (for example, notice or registration) providing that the work contained a notice reserving these rights. Thereby, the notice "All Rights Reserved" was born.

14. Can I protect my recipe under copyright?

A simple listing of ingredients is not protected under copyright law. However, where a recipe or formula is accompanied by substantial literary expression in the form of an explanation or directions, or when there is a collection of recipes as in a cookbook, there may be basis for copyright protection.

15. Can I copyright my mother's diary I found in her attic?

You can register copyright in the diary only if you are the transferee (by will or inheritance). Copyright is the right of the author of the work or the author's heirs or assignees, not of the one who only owns or possesses the physical work itself.

16. Can a minor claim copyright?

Minors may claim copyright, and the copyright Office does issue registrations to minors, but state laws may regulate the business dealings involving copyrights owned by minors.

17. Can I use a stage name or a pen name for copyrighting?

There is no legal requirement that the author be identified by his or her real name on the application form. If filing under a fictitious name, check the "Pseudonymous" box at space 2.

18. Does my work have to be published to be protected?

Publication is not necessary for copyright protection.

19. Can I copyright a name, title, slogan or logo?

Copyright does not protect names, titles, slogans, or short phrases. In some cases, these items may be protected under trademark law. However, copyright protection may be available for logo art work that contains sufficient authorship. Additionally, in some circumstances, an artistic logo may also be protected as a trademark.

20. What are the Copyright Office registration procedures?

For original registration: Again, to register a work, send the following three elements in the same envelope or package to:

Library of Congress
Copyright Office
101 Independence Avenue, S.E.
Washington, D.C. 20559-6000

- A properly completed application form
- A nonrefundable filing fee of $30 for each application.*
- A no returnable deposit of the work being registered.

21. Does the Copyright office have a website?

Need more detailed information visit: www.copyright.gov or for details subject to change (price, deposit requirements, etc.)

SUMMARY

Well that's what I considered the high points of basic copyrighting. In the large scheme of things there's probably no one lurking around that wants to willfully steal your story or writing but on the other hand it is wise to be knowledgeable and alert. Now go be wise, know your rights, respect the rights of others and write for the joy of it!

Chapter 10

BOOK MARKETING WITH A PLAN

Very few authors get rich selling their books. I hate to be the one to break the news to you. But I felt I must be honest. Many writers set themselves up for failure by having wrong expectations.

The reason successful authors and publishers embrace a plan (program) is because they know it is highly unlikely they will get rich from direct sales of their book.

They know writing and publishing a book will change their lives. But they realize most of the rewards will come from sources other than publishing their own book.

You must realize your book is a product and as a product it has to be marketed. Your plan provides a map for everything you do afterwards.

KNOW THE DIFFERENCE FROM YOUR PLAN AND PROPOSAL

Your book marketing plan is what I often describe as your map. It describes your book, what you will do after the book is completed and published. It also describes who you hope to sell your book to – *target audience*. We talk more about that a little later in this chapter. So in short you can say your book marketing plan is your roadmap to success and profits.

Your book proposal is a sales (direct-marketing) document with a sole purpose. It's single purpose is to convince a publisher that your book will earn a profit, if published.

The proposal should focus on the size and buying power of the targeted market you will attract, the problem your book solves, how your book plans to solve the problem, how different your book is from others already published on the subject and how you plan to promote your book.

> "Your book proposal is a sales (direct-marketing) document with a sole purpose."

If you have selected a traditional method of publishing, you can and should develop your proposal before you even write your book. It will help solidify and crystallize some of your ideas. In fact, how well you develop your proposal including a detailed table of contents or chapter outline in your proposal, the easier and faster you can get started mining your ideas, creating a structure and writing your book.

IDENTIFY YOUR TARGETED MARKET

Why do people buy non-fiction books? Most readers buy books to solve problems or help with fulfilling a need. For example, when I first started speaking for a fee I went out and bought a couple of popular books about speaking.

When browsing in the bookstore, I was attracted to Lilyan Wilder's book "7 Steps to Fearless Speaking" I read the back cover. I noticed she could help with 7 easy steps. I skimmed the table of contents, read a few lines and immediately liked her easy to read style. It went in my purchase basket.

Because I wanted to hear from several authorities on the subject, I picked up another book by Nido R. Qubein, "How to Be a Great Communicator: In Person on Paper, and on the Podium. His style of writing was not as easy to read but it still went in my purchase basket as well. Which brings us back to my original point; people buy non-fiction books to solve problems. To identify your targeted market, pinpoint a problem they have and the solution of course.

Problems come in all shapes and sizes. Usually a general category problem applies to all types of markets.

- *Hobbies.* Is your tennis game, golf game, bridge game as good as you'd like? Are you considering taking up horse-back riding? Want to improve your computer skills? What ever the case may be, your desire to improve or change your level of performance is considered the problem.

- *Health.* The first thing anyone does when your doctor diagnose your cholesterol is high and you need to lose 20 pounds. You go look for a book that will walk you through step by step to lose weight or lower cholesterol. You turn to someone that has solved the problem to learn from their experience.

- *Mental State.* Are you feeling stressful about the economy? Are you noticing unexplained physical symptoms possibly related to stress? Once again, you have a problem and you are looking for a solution in book form. Someone who has outlined easy steps or ways to de-stress in our society.

- *Personal Finance.* Worried about lay-offs, down-sizing, retirement? Books that offer financial solutions to economic problems during shaky times are guaranteed to succeed.

- *Marketing.* We live in a competitive society. Small business owners and managers everywhere need a growing database of customers and clients. Therefore, they seek out how to books that offers solutions on improving their advertising copy, improving their business image or their website.

Each of the problem categories describes a problem and a need for a solution. The main goal of your marketing plan and the Write Your Best Book Now program is to identify the problem your book solves and then present the solution. The more intense the problem and the easier you can make your solution, the more readers will seek out your book.

Your task becomes to re-structure your knowledge into bite-size reader solutions. Appeal to the masses, by letting them know what's in it for them and how easy the solution is with your book. For example, let's consider the book title I mentioned earlier about speaking.

The title could have been: *"How to Overcome Your Fear of Speaking"* instead of *"7 Steps to Fearless Speaking"* The latter is more appealing because it alludes to only 7 steps to my solution.

TARGET YOUR NICHE

Which brings me to our next tip, "Target Your Niche" Identifying a niche is really hot in the marketing world right now and rightly so.

After you have defined a problem and solution, researched your competition, you now have to develop a different approach. With all the books in the world on your topic, it's not enough to know the solution; you have to present the solution in a different way than existing books do.

You need to develop a way of making your book different. You need a different viewpoint, a niche, and a different spin on perhaps the same information. Examine the problem again and the solution your book solves with the goal of devising a way to describe and present your knowledge in a different way than existing books. Here are several ways you to do this:

- *Market Segment.* You can develop a niche by focusing on an occupation, sex, or age group, i.e. Lose 14 Pounds in 2 Weeks: A Guide for Women Above 40, Lose Weight Safely Before, During & After Pregnancy.

- *Broadening Market.* Consider appealing to a broader

market: Lose 14 Pounds in 14 Days: A Guide for Working Class Men & Women.

- *Focus.* Attack a big problem by emphasizing a particular tool or technique that you have experience with. For example, show how heart attack survivors can lose 14 pounds in 2 weeks by eating only fish, white meats and walking 10 miles a day.

- *Program.* I love this one. Base your solution on the way you solve a large problem by breaking it into steps, i.e. Write Your Best Book Now: An 8 Step Program for book writing.

- *Expertise.* Base your niche on your market's previous experience with a topic, i.e. The Last Business Book You'll Ever Need!

- *Goal.* Organize your existing information around benefits of achieving the goal: Free Again, Healthy Again!

- *Affinity.* Perhaps you have a relationship with a high visibility organization that has benefited from your ideas; you can reframe your knowledge by leveraging off your association: The Bank of America Financial Program or the Southern Methodist University Weight Loss Program.

You may have noticed in each one of the above examples of the same market, the contents of the book would probably be the same! The books would contain the same basic ideas, suggestions, tips, etc.

For example, all the books about diets would probably stress the importance of eating right, choosing the right foods in right portions and daily exercise. Yet, each book presents a different viewpoint targeting a different market.

So have no fear about approaching the same subject as existing books. Focus in on your unique ideas and viewpoint. Remember, according to the writer of Ecclesiastes, "There's nothing new under the sun." Bernice Fitz–Gibbon said so eloquently, "Creativity often consists of merely turning up what is already there. Did you know that right and left shoes were only thought up only little more than a century ago."

DEVELOP A PROMOTION PLAN

Promote passionately while you write. There are two aspects to developing your promotion plan. Realize it begins the day you start writing and never ends. The other is the more you write the better you become at it. You need to begin building name recognition in your field. In other words, you want to begin developing your public image.

No I'm not suggesting you become a politician but I am saying you must get involved in your book's promotion. After all, you are the one that cares the most for your project. Many authors and especially small business owners/authors dread book promotion like a plague. With all that I already do, I jumped the hurdle of writing and completing my book, now I have to promote it as well –arggh.

Yet, book promotion is not an activity most publishers are accomplished at either. You, as the author - the one who believes - the most in your message, have to take responsibility for promoting your book. Publishers are like factories producing printed books or distributors delivering boxes of books to bookstores. So don't believe the myth that a publisher is going to promote your book.

Unless your name already has tons of acclaim, most publishers will do little or no advertising of your book. They may send out a limited number of press releases and review copies but often depend on the catalogs they send out twice a year to bookstore buyers.

> "The economies of book publishing allow a book publisher to actively market a book for 30 to 90 days, and then it depends on word of mouth."
> —*Spencer Johnson*

In an interview when asked about the success of his last books, Spencer Johnson whose book "Who Moved My Cheese" stayed on the best seller list five years after its release with more than 14 million copies sold and counting said, "The economies of book publishing allow a book publisher to actively market a book for 30 to 90 days, then it depends on word of mouth."

It's not just the agent or the advertising, though those things help. In the end, the book has to resonate with people's hearts and heads." With all that in mind, it's no surprise why your publisher is more than likely not going to be able to do your book justice and the real promoting will fall to you. You have more to gain than the publisher in the success of your book. Therefore, your book marketing plan should include:

- *Media.* Magazines, newsletters and newspapers which you can submit to for free. It's o.k. to get paid, if you must but you are most importantly after the exposure.

- *Community groups.* Offer to speak for your community for free. Gain the exposure you need; then perhaps other groups will begin to ask you and be most willing to pay.

- *Associations.* Many sponsor conventions and trade shows where you can speak or serve on a panel.

Develop a list of contacts and offer them your free articles that combine your knowledge that focuses on their organization's needs.

Develop your website. If you don't have one that focuses on your book or you as an individual, create one. Your website is now one of the first places agents, publishers and clients will look to find out more about you. The better quality it is, the more it will pre-sell your book proposal or your book itself. First impressions are important. Make your website a good one that accurately reflects you as an individual.

During the planning stage of your book don't forget to include the passion points designed to sell your book. One of those passion points is to identify and contact the influencers in your field. As early as possible, send them your book's table of contents and two sample chapters.

The two sample chapters and table of contents help prove your commitment and intention to complete your book project. Make it your biggest goal to have a "name" or trusted authority in your field endorse your book by either providing a brief quote or testimonial for the front or back cover.

One good way of approaching an established authority is to interview them. This establishes at least a dialog with them. In the process of interviewing, at the opportune moment you can ask for a quote or even an overview/introduction for your book project. Some might ask for a symbolic honorarium but most will be pleased to write a brief overview or testimonial for your book project because it further promotes them in their endeavors.

Beyond quotes, your book marketing plan should include a list of review copies of your book for possible mention, review in their publication or website.

IDENTIFY FOLLOW-UP INCOME

This section of your marketing plan is last because it can only be accomplished after your book is published whether by traditional means or self-published. After your book is released, the opportunities will be available. Yet, we are including in the book marketing plan for it will influence the way your book is developed, the way you prepare your proposal and contract for traditional publishing.

We noted earlier in the chapter, that the majority of your book profits will come from the doors and opportunities that the book opens for you. It's what the publishing industry calls the "back end" sales that will buy your vacation in the Bahamas, not advances or royalties.

> "It's what the publishing industry calls the 'back end' sales that will buy your vacation in the Bahamas, not advances or royalties."

We'll start by identifying your profit centers and passive income sources you plan to develop from your published book. These will center on publications and services that you offer through your website. That's why it's important that your publishing contract allow you the freedom to mention your website as much as appropriate. Follow-up income opportunities may include:

- *Audio Cassettes.* Don't expect to get wealthy from them. But audio cassettes will permit you to gain extra mileage from your speeches.

- *E-Books.* These are short 10-70 page books that you write and format using your word-processor software or a desktop publishing program. After formatting, you use the Acrobat program to convert them into a PDF format (Portable Document Format), which allows you to sell and distribute them as downloadable files from your website or as email attachments. E-books can offer detailed treatment of specific topics that were only lightly touched upon in your original print book.

- *Personal Services.* You should set your website up to help promote and leverage the expertise you displayed by writing your book. One on one coaching and corporate consulting are two aspects to consider. You can develop and present seminars and workshops. Also, you can explore the opportunity of developing a curriculum you distribute as electronic files. Or you may develop a profitable speaking career launched from the success of your book.

- *Workbooks.* Another form of e-books, that expands on your book's topic allowing readers to relate your ideas to their specific tasks. They usually contain guided tutorials, checklists, worksheets and progress-trackers that would have slowed the pace down in your original book.

The quicker you include follow-up income opportunities in your thinking, the easier it will be to write your book in a way that promotes these opportunities.

SUMMARY

The publishing world and our society have changed. Writing and publishing your book can still change your life. But now a book is not the be-all and end-all, it is simply a tool that allows you to become a more successful business person, taking the profitable road to success and destiny.

Chapter 11

TOP 40 INCOME STREAMS TO CREATE FROM YOUR BOOK

Would you like to create life long passive income? Income streams that produce like the Energizer™ bunny, going and going and going. You can do it; just use the principles below to create multiple income streams for you and your family.

Even after you finish your book manuscript new ideas will probably continue to surface. Ideas that you wish you had thought to include in your book. Instead of going back to re-work your manuscript, consider using them in your promotional material or turn it into an informational product. Become a trusted resource and supplier of fresh information in your field.

Continue to develop your topic by creating articles, speeches, workshops, courses, or invite readers to submit questions and suggestions to your website. Develop your topic and title into a brand that produces increasing amounts of income through your personal services and/or information products.

Sounds like a good idea, right? Now you should decide on how to re-package your book content to make it salable. Depending on your market, some packaging will sell better than others. For example, you can re-package your information in a series of information products, package it in an ebook, manual, report or newsletter, put it on CDs or present it at seminars. You can focus on one area, or utilize many areas.

One thing is certain; people are paying billions of dollars to obtain well packaged information! There are books that sell for up to $100 and more, with manuals in a close second. There are e-reports that consist of 10-12 pages selling for up to $97 or more, while seminars can cost as much as $15,000 for a single weekend.

Are you getting excited yet? It may sound incredible to the average person, but people are willing to pay top dollar for information. However, the "packaging" must be perceived as being worth the price you are asking. So before you run off to re-package your book, first decide on how to package your information. Consider who your primary audience is, and cater to those people in everything you do.

> "One thing is certain; people are paying billions of dollars to obtain well packaged information!"

This is where you stop thinking of your book as just a book. You must begin to think in terms of "content." Think back to your book outline you created and the research you did and the tons of information you collected. That body of information is your "content."

The way you packaged and presented it will now change. You can change the way you packaged your content in multiple ways. By doing so, you can create multiple profit streams by re-packaging, slicing and chunking your original content.

Just begin to slice your 'content' into blogs, articles, website(s), ebooks, reports, pod casts and much more. Explore, create and prosper! Here are the top 40 ways to re-package your book content and create new profit streams:

1. *E-Books.* Excerpt or Expand book content; compile into a PDF file, text, HTML or EXE file. Look for a free way to convert content to a PDF file in the Resource Section of

this book. Additionally, if you need further information on how to create, sell and promote your book as an ebook go to http://www.clickeasyebooks.com

2. *Booklets - Tips/How to.* Select tips or task related to your book or excerpt content to place in booklet. Condense material to around 20-24 booklet pages. Convert to a PDF file and send to a printer. Or use home office laser printer to duplex print your booklet. Visit Resource Section of book for more about booklet making and printing.

> "Just begin to slice your 'content' into blogs, articles, website(s), ebooks, reports, pod casts and much more. Explore, create and prosper!"

3. *Articles.* Again, you can excerpt or write fresh material on the same subject as your book. Pull from all the information gathered during your research process. Then use these articles to market your book. They will spread all over and began to create a fresh stream of books sales or pump up existing sales. Need help developing your articles? Visit the *Article Marketing Speedway* website http://articlespeedway.net for resources and tips.

4. *Ezine/Newsletters.* Use your newly developed articles and excerpts in an offline or an online ezine. Your book could easily yield enough content for a year's worth of newsletters.

5. *Blogs.* Additionally, your articles can be chunked into short paragraphs or content snippets for your blog. Snippets are usually developed by taking the title and first paragraph or two from an article.

6. *Audio Books.* Audio books are easy. Simply record yourself (or someone else) reading your book content. Yup, just read, record and you've got an audio book.

> *Resource Tip:* Visit our resource section at the end of this ebook for a free software product to record your audio book.

7. *Pod cast.* Record yourself talking about your book topic. You may read part of your book (sections or chapters of content.) Or you can just talk about it. Remember, you are the expert now. Just let it flow; talk about what you know. You can use the free software product I referred to in #6 to record your pod cast.

8. *Audio Program.* When you do research and gather content for a book idea, you almost always have more information than you can fit into one book. A one CD 'audio book' can easily become a full length audio program by breaking it into separate CDs for each chapter.

9. *Vlogcast.* A vlogcast is just like a blog or podcast except you record the content as a video instead of audio or text.

> *Resource Tip:* The software to edit and package video is completely free. Visit our resource section for the details. Please know this software does not include a web cam. You will have to invest in a digital video or web cam camera.

10. *Video Program.* For your video program, read the book into the camera or video yourself teaching the material to a group. Again, like the audio program break the content up into sections and place each section on a separate DVD.

11. *Workbooks.* Re-examine your book content and create a workbook, study guide or report specifically designed to teach the material. Format the information in a summarized style and add questions for each book chapter or section.

12. *Multi-Media Kits.* Compile your multi-media kit by putting your book, audio book and/or DVDs together.

13. *Coaching Program.* Present your book content via email or phone according to how you've structured your coaching program.

14. *Teleseminars.* Present your book content via the phone (telebridge connection) in an interview format. If you can make it interesting enough you can easily present it like a speech with q/a determined before the call. The telebridge connection is similar to the old party lines.

15. *Teleworkshops.* Teleworkshops are presented via telephone in a workbook type style. This works best with a smaller group so the participants can be interactive.

16. *Home Study Course.* Combine your book, audio programs and/or video programs, workbooks, etc. into one product.

17. *Membership Site.* Include your text, audio and video content in a password protected website where your clients pay you each month for access to the material. Don't forget a membership site can be an opportunity for monthly income.

18. *Radio Show.* With the new age power of the Internet practically anyone can host their own radio show. Use the same content you used for your podcast. Simply, record your book content in an interesting format. Have the pre-recorded version played at various times or host a live show.

19. *TV Show.* Internet TV (IPTV) is rapidly moving toward us. Just like Internet radio – at the time of this writing, within 1-2 years anyone can build their own TV show on the Internet.

20. *Syndicated Column.* As your fame grows in your field, you may be asked to submit your articles to a newspaper. Or again, use the power of the Internet to post your articles on your own web site so others can syndicate.

21. *Mini Books or Reports.* Take one chapter from your book,

add content, illustrations, case studies and transform into a mini-book or report. Or consider using your chapters 'as is'. If your book has 5 chapters, you could make it into 5 'special reports.' These little gems make great gifts to give your website visitors a sample of your book.

22. *CD/DVD Training.* Those CDs and/or video DVDs we talked about earlier. You could use them to create a monthly training subscription service. Like 'Video Professor' you can monthly send your product. Remember, you already have the content created – now get your clients to pay you monthly for it.

23. *Magazine.* Consider developing your content into a magazine. A magazine is nothing but a large glossy Newsletter. One of the great things about a magazine is you can get advertisers to pay you money each month to be listed in your magazine.

24. *Software.* Compile your book content into an executable file and it becomes software. It then can be promoted with a higher perceived value. You don't have to be a software developer. Many ebook compiler software delivers the ability to combine (package) text, audio and video into an EXE.

25. *Keynote Speaking.* O.k. your book is done. You're the expert. Now brush up on your speaking skills; summarize your book content into PowerPoint slides and speak well.

26. *Resell Rights.* Provide others the ability to resell your book and keep 100% of the profits. I must tell you there are pros and cons. Pro: Higher perceived value. Con: You lose control of your product. If you want extra income – this is a great way to get it. But if you don't want to lose control of your book – don't do this.

27. *Private Label Rights.* This has gained popularity over the years on the Internet. You provide others the ability to modify your content. Brand it with their name and resell

it as their own. Again, there's a pro and con. Pro: Higher perceived value (you can charge more.) Con: It will no longer be your product after it's re-branded.

28. *Licensing.* You could make an arrangement with an individual or company to purchase a large quantity of your product. For example, a company may license your book for all their employees.

29. *Foreign Rights.* You could tap into foreign markets by converting your book into other languages.

30. *Consulting.* You deliver a culmination of all your research and content presented as required by the person and/or company that hires you. Or give simply give your customers advice on topics related to your book. You can consult via e-mail, message board or chat room.

31. *Checklist.* Create a list of things to check for a particular process related to your book's topic. Ex.: a checklist of things to consider when choosing a POD publisher.

32. *Templates.* Design a template that will make a certain action easier for your readers. Ex.: a template for writing a newsletter.

33. *Transcripts.* Create an ebook of text transcripts of a related live event. Ex.: seminar, speech, class, interview, etc.

34. *Dictionary of Terms.* Publish a web directory or ebook dictionary of terms related to your specific book's topic.

35. *Advice Column.* Offer an email consultation or a live chat room q/a where you give your web site visitors and customers advice on your book's topic.

36. *Plans.* Create ready-made plans for a particular project your book's targeted audience wants to accomplish. It could be a diet plan, marketing plan, landscape plan, etc.

37. *Private Web Site.* Give access to a private part of your web site where customers can find helpful information non-customers can't access.

38. *Directory of Resources.* Compile a list offline and online resources. You could include names, phone numbers, addresses, web sites and email addresses.

39. *Mentor Program.* Give your customers limited or unlimited consulting with their purchase. Allow them to contact you by e-mail, phone, fax, in person, etc.

40. Email Lessons. Teach a class via e-mail about your book's topic or a subject your customers want to learn. Email them study materials, worksheets, assignments, etc.

The main thing about re-packaging your book is you do whatever meets your need. If you need something to spread your message and book like wild fire, then create a viral product. Use a viral package like a podcast, special report, etc. If you are just starting and need an entry-level product then develop an e-book, e-report or audio book.

If you want to create a high dollar product to complement your book—then compile a group of products together like books, CDs, Workbooks, DVDs, etc. Notice that all of the products above flow from your original book's information and content. There is no difference between the content in your ebook, audio and video except the way you choose to package it. Remember, you could receive a much higher profit because you have provided a higher value to your client.

SUMMARY

You've already accomplished the hard part; you wrote your important message down in book form. Now go multiply your book profits with new income streams.

Appendix I

QUICKSTART GUIDE FOR SELF PUBLISHING

.

STEP ONE
Self Publishing Education

As with any business venture you must educate yourself to have the best possible chance of success. There are lots of misinformation and misunderstandings of self-publishing in general. Education is a powerful piece of the 'Success Pie.' You wouldn't dream of becoming a book writer without first learning about book writing.

The aspect of Book Publishing is no different. This book about Self Publishing is one of the best starting places for your publishing education currently being offered to the self publisher. Remember, Knowledge is Power. If you are reading this book, your self publishing education starts here.

Know your options. Discover the difference between vanity publishers, subsidy publishers, book packagers, pod publishers and self-publishing.

The term *vanity publisher* in general, refers to the publisher (sometimes called a book producer) who prints and binds a book in medium to large quantities at the author's sole expense.

On the other hand, a *subsidy publisher* considered (a joint venture publisher, a co-op publisher, or a partner publisher) also takes payment from the author to print and bind a book. Unlike the vanity publisher, they may contribute a portion of the cost, as well as adjunct services such as editing, distribution, warehousing, and some degree of marketing.

Book packaging is different than subsidy or vanity publishing. Some companies as their business specialize in it. A book packager serves as an independent contractor to produce a predetermined number of your books. All the books belong to you. Book packagers work for a pre-set fee, and all the profits are yours.

POD publishing is exactly what it says: Publish on Demand. This means that books are printed when someone orders them, and they aren't printed unless someone orders them. After the books are printed and sold usually quarterly the POD publisher pays the author royalties from their book sales. They aren't stocked (except in minute quantities) in distributor warehouses. Which is for the most part a good thing except when bookstores look them up on their databases they often find that they have to be "backordered?"

The term *Self Publishing* is most commonly used to discuss publishing that is handled completely by the author. Self-publishing requires the author to undertake the entire cost of publication him/herself. The writer would handle all marketing, distribution, storage, etc.

It must be made clear; self publishing implies that "you" are the "publisher". In fact, ownership of the ISBN determines who the publisher is. If you didn't buy your ISBN's directly from RR Bowker, you don't own them. If you do not own the ISBN, you are NOT considered a self publisher in the publishing world.

STEP TWO
Self Publishing Preparation

The preparation stage of the self-publishing process includes everything you need to do to your book manuscript before taking it to the book printer. This includes determining your publishing goals. Like do you plan to sell your personal family history book to a few friends and family or do you plan to mass market your book to the world. After deciding your market then you prepare your book using the important steps below:

1. *Write a Business Plan*
This is where book publishing journey begins. Remember, you don't have to start with a 30 page document. But do draft an

outline of all the costs that you will have in the self publishing process.

Include costs before publication, after publication and everything from start up costs to the shipping price of mailing a book. This is the point you decide whether you should print a small quantity of books for friends and family or establish a small publishing company by purchasing a block of ISBNs.

2. Get ISBN Numbers.

Remember this is what identifies you as a book publisher. It is the only way you can be considered a self-publisher in the publishing industry. At the time of this writing, no one can give, assign or sell you ISBNs except RR Bowker, the U.S. ISBN agency.

3. Invest in Book Editing.

Invest in your book; get it professionally edited. Copy or line editing will bring your manuscript up to professional standards. Don't settle for having your family member take a look at your manuscript.

4. Hire a Book Designer for Book Layout.

The book layout is what structures the content of your book and makes it look like a book. Again invest in your book project, this is not the time to settle for any thing less than a professional look. If your book looks sloppy, it will limit its success in the market.

5. Consider Do-It-Yourself Layout Options

If your budget is a shoestring or you are a die hard do-it-yourselfer, you might consider purchasing a book template software like Book Design Wizard (see the Resource Rolodex at the end of this book.) You simply input your text, images, book specs and the software will generate a professional layout for submission to your printer.

6. Thinking of Other Do It Yourself Layout Options

If budget is not a major concern, then you may consider investing in Pagemaker or InDesign software for your book layout projects.

The price is a little steep at $400 to $699 at Adobe's website. Also, you may encounter a learning curve but there are good templates that will shorten it for you. Either way you decide, make your book the best it can be. Your readers will love you for it and proudly refer your book to all their friends.

7. Create Bound Galleys for Reviews.

Bound Galleys are limited run book proofs, often unedited, generally used to get book reviews before the publication date of your book. Additionally, bound galleys do not have a laminated full color cover.

8. Get Your Book Proof Read.

Some are tempted to skip this step in preparing their book for publication. My advice is don't skip this step. A book full of errors can cost you in sales later on--including loss of respect for your work.

Proof reading is not the same as editing; it is done after the book designer formats or lays out your book into pages. The proofreader looks particularly at word breaks and sentence layout. Some minor corrections missed in the first line edit may also be made.

9. Invest in Cover Design.

Seventy-five percent of 300 booksellers surveyed (half from independent bookstores and half from chains) identified the look and design of the book cover as the most important component. They agreed that the jacket is prime real estate for promoting a book. On that note, your book cover design can make or brake your book marketing campaign. So, I encourage you to get your book cover professionally designed.

10. Considering Do It Yourself Book Cover Options

We're taught to not judge a book by its cover in life. Yet, we all do it. So realistically, a book is judged by its cover in the publishing world. If you want your book to have the best chance of success in a professional market, don't drop the ball here. Another option for the do-it-yourselfer to get a professional look is the *Book Cover Pro* software (see the Resource Rolodex at the end of this book.)

STEP THREE
Self Publishing Book Printing

According to how far along you are in your self-publishing process, you may know this already. Most printers can print books although most printers are not book printers. With that said, the question becomes can they print your book in a way that's cost effective for you. Additionally, don't forget to consider the option of direct pod publishing with Lighting Source, a subsidiary of Ingram. You essentially submit your fully prepared book to them for printing and some distribution. See Chapter 7 page 48 for the details. I've listed below some options for your book's trim size.

1. SINGLE COLOR TRADE PAPERBACK AND HARDCOVER -
Standard Book Sizes

a. Mass Market Paperback – 4¼ X 7"
This trim size used to be called dime novels. Because the large publishing houses print this size in tens of thousands it's tough to compete in small quantities. Also, the perceived value of this size is lower than the other book sizes. Choose this size cafefully.

b. Trade Paperback and Hardcover – 5½ X 8½"
Its the most popular trim size for fiction and non-fiction books. If you are planning for a quanity above 500 copies it doesn't make any difference whether you use this size or the trade paperback alternate size of 6 x 9. If you plan to print quantities under 500 copies, choose this trim (actually 5¼ X 8¼"). It is significantly less expensive than the 6X9 alternate with no lower perceived value.

c. Trade Paperback and Hardcover alternate – 6 X 9"
This was considered the standard trade paperback size for years before the Internet printing press. This size fits perfectly on a 25 X 38 standard size sheet of paper. This is now the standard

Internet printing press book trim size. If you are printing quantities above 500 copies, this is the recommended trim size.

d. *Textbook Paperback and Hardcover – 7 X 10"*
This is considered standard size for text books and other "how-to" books. It is best in quantities above 500 copies because it fits the Internet printing press perfectly. Under 500 copies yields the same pricing as 8½ X 11" only you trim off the excess paper.

e. Workbook – 8½ X 11"
It is considered a standard workbook trim size. Printing under 500 copies you're dealing with a slightly smaller trim size (8¼ X 10¾) because of the digital equipment standards. Over 500 copies fits traditional Internet printing press. Its hard to compete with large publishers in this size for the same reason as the Mass Market size.

2. COLOR ILLUSTRATED PAPERBACK AND HARDCOVER -
Illustrated Children's Books, Art Books, Travel and How-to Books

a. Hardcover and Paperback 8 X 8"
Standard children's book size. Not recommended for paperback children's books in low quantities. The competition is too tough from traditional children's book publishers. OK size as hardcover children's book or as paperback for non-illustrated children's books. Pricing is available with or without book jacket.

b. Hardcover & Paperback 8 X 10"
Very standard children's book size. Like the 8 X 8, not recommended in paperback for children's illustrated books. Pricing is available with or without book jacket.

c. Hardcover & Paperback – Oblong 10 X 8"
Standard children's book size. Not recommended in paperback for children's books but great as hardcover. Common paperback size for non-children's picture books. Pricing is available with or without book jacket.

STEP FOUR
Self-Publishing Distribution

At the time of this writing there are no perfect distribution channels for the self-published book. Looking for the perfect book distribution channel is like searching for the pot of gold at the end of the rainbow.

Unless you have a detailed marketing plan and a good amount of money working for you, and in many cases, access to media and traditional bookstore distribution, you may be headed for disappointing sales. Don't get me wrong; I'm not predicting you won't be successful. But I am saying it will most likely be like swimming against the tide trying to distribute and market books in a traditional manner.

Here's another good reason to consider POD publishing or printing your book through the Lighting Source company. Your pod published book will be included in the Ingram database as a POD title. This one program will make your book available to a network of 20,000 retail stores including Amazon.com and BN.com. This inexpensive distribution is a good starting place for getting your books in the bookstores.

STEP FIVE
Self-Publishing Marketing

1. Push Button Easy Book Marketing
Ready to get those books stacked in your garage into the hands of even MORE readers? Earma has harnessed the power of internet promotion into one place to set your book ablaze with new sales. Get the ebook Push Button Easy Book Marketing Strategies with software bonuses that help you promote your book to a new market - the WORLD. Visit the website http://bookmarketinghelp.com for resources and tips.

2. 1001 Ways to Market Your Book

If you haven't done so already you need to buy a copy of this book. Some of the information is a little dated but for under $30 a great place to start.

3. Book Author Website Design & Development

Implementing this is a must if you have any hope of being successful selling your self published book online. It's your way of telling the "world" about your book. Visit Scribere Creative http://scriberecreative.com for author websites and services.

4. Online Bookstores

The perfect "first step" for selling your book and/or ebook on the Internet is to list your book in available online book stores.

5. Press Release Service

Promote Your Business with Professional and Affordable PR Services including placement on News. Google, Yahoo!, Reuters, and thousands more, starting at only $69! Visit Send2Press.com for details.

6. RR Bowker/Book Marketing Works

Direct Sales to the non-bookstore market. They generate the leads and you make the sales calls or they generate the leads and they make the sales calls. Visit website below for details http://www.bookmarketingworks.com/.

Appendix II

150 INSPIRING SELF STARTERS IN SELF PUBLISHING

You never know where your dream will take you until you take the leap of faith. Most successful publishers didn't start that way. They started with a hope or a promise but never a guarantee. Are you ready to join the circle of successfully published authors? Read these inspiring snippet stories and self-publish NOW. For now really is better than later.

1. Terry McMillan, best-selling author of Waiting to Exhale and How Stella Got Her Groove Back, published her first novel, Mama. Many of her novels have been made into movies as well.

2. Peter McWilliams indie published many of his New York Times best selling books, including Life 101, Do It, Wealth 101, The Personal Computer Book, The Personal Computer in Business Book, and others.

3. In 1851, Herman Melville wrote a letter to Nathaniel Hawthorne complaining about his monetary problems. Yet, he still self-published his classic novel Moby Dick, who many consider the greatest novel ever written by an American.

4. Bruce Lansky, now publisher of Meadowbrook Press, has written or edited many of the company's best-selling titles, including The Best Baby Name Book (3.5 million copies sold), 15,000+ Baby Names (1.5 million copies sold), The Very Best Baby Name Book (950,000 copies sold), and 35,000+ Baby Names (1 million copies sold).

5. Phil Laut sold more than 200,000 copies of his self-published book, Money Is My Friend. He went on to sell mass-market rights to Ballantine Books and foreign

rights to Germany, Serbia-Croatia, South Korea, Iceland, Spain, France, and the Netherlands.

6. Deborah Lawrenson originally self-published her novel, The Art of Falling. This combination of wartime love story and contemporary heroine searching for the truth about her father was later sold to Arrow Books for publication in the summer of 2005.

7. Medard Laz self-published the first 5,000 copies of Love Adds a Little Chocolate, a collection of 100 stories to brighten your day. He then sold the rights to Warner Books, which went on to sell hundreds of thousands of copies.

8. In 2004, former star running back Robert Smith of the Minnesota Vikings self-published his biography, The Rest of the Iceberg: An Insider's View on the World of Sport and Celebrity. Not able to find a traditional publisher, he self-published through Ink Water Books, a print-on-demand company. Smith turned down a $20 million contract to continue playing when he retired from professional football in 2001.

9. Robert Smyth started Yellow Moon Press in 1978 by publishing a book of his poetry. Since then he has published 53 titles on the art of oral tradition and spoken word as it relates to storytelling, poetry, and music. He has published Robert Bly, Ruth Stone, Coleman Barks, Rafe Martin, Gioia Timpanelli and other storytellers.

10. Scott Adams, creator of the Dilbert comic strip and book series, self-published an original ebook, God's Debris, early in 2001 as a way of testing the market for a new book. As a result, he was able to get an 'unusually good deal' from his regular publisher, Andrews McMeel, when he sold them the book rights.

11. In 1998, Arthur Agatston, author of The South Beach

Diet, began by self-publishing several hundred pamphlets outlining his diet ideas for patients. Several years later, with the help of an agent, he sold rights to Rodale. Within a year, the book had sold almost seven million copies.

12. Julie Aigner-Clark founded the Baby Einstein company to produce early-learning videos, DVDs, and audio CDs for babies and toddlers. Many of the products feature poems written by her. The company has won many awards for its products and has sold more than 8 million copies of its videos and other products. In November 2001, she and her husband sold the company to Disney for $25 million.

13. Nigerian writer Christopher Albani was jailed in his home country for publishing some of his books. A number of his books were banned in Nigeria before he sold right to his first U.S. novel, GraceLand, to Farrar Straus Giroux with the aide of agent Sandy Dijkstra.

14. Craig Alesse began Amherst Media by self-publishing his own how-to photography books. His company is now one of the premiere how-to photography publishing companies in the world, distributing to photography stores across the country.

15. Debbie Allen sold 40,000 copies of her Confessions of Shameless Self Promoters and then sold reprint rights to McGraw-Hill. In addition, she sold rights to a new book, Positively Fearless Selling, to Dearborn Trade. An international speaker and consultant, she helps businesses to out-market, out-sell, and out-profit their competition.

16. Todd McFarlane formed Image Comics with six fellow artists and proceeded to self-publish the Spawn comic book in 1992. The first issue sold 1.7 million copies!

17. Linda Watanabe McFerrin and her travel writer friends from the Wild Writing Women group self-published a

collection of their wilder stories — about voodoo and bus accidents and pants lost while climbing. The collection, Wild Writing Women: Stories of World Travel, sold out before the book was even printed.

18. In 1966, poet and songwriter Rod McKuen self-published his first major book, Stanyon Street and Other Sorrows, via his company, Stanyan Music. He sold 40,000 copies before Random House picked it up.

19. Marc Allen, publisher of New World Library, chose to publish his own book, Visionary Business, after publishing many other bestselling titles, including Creative Visualization by Shakti Gawain, The Seven Spiritual Laws of Success by Deepak Chopra, and The Power of Now by Eckhart Tolle.

20. In 1962, trumpeter Herb Alpert and his partner Jerry Moss formed A&M records with $100 apiece. One of the first albums they produced was the gold-selling Herb Alpert & The Tijuana Brass's White Cream & Other Delights, a classic record of the mid-60s. They built A&M into the nation's largest record company not owned by a conglomerate before finally selling out to Polygram in 1989 for $500 million.

21. Judith Appelbaum originally self-published How to Get Happily Published, then sold the rights to Harper Collins. The book has now been through many editions and has sold more than 500,000 copies.

22. Mary Appelhof self-published Worms Eat My Garbage. Her first edition sold more than 100,000 copies. In 1997, she published her second edition.

23. Beginning her book career by self-publishing her first book of poetry, Justice: Just Us, Just Me, on August 23, 1999, Mary B. Morrison had been writing poetry since 1983. In 2000, after self-publishing and selling 10,000

copies of her novel, Soul Mates Dissipate, Mary B. Morrison sold rights to Kensington for a six-figure advance.

24. Viggo Mortensen is not just an actor who starred in the Lord of the Rings trilogy, but he is also a publishing entrepreneur with a direct-mail operation, Perceval Press, that he launched in 2002. He's been retailing his 20-title list both online (several of the books are by Mortensen) and via direct mail.

25. John Muir founded the company that bears his name in order to self-publish his multi-million copy bestseller, How to Keep Your Volkswagen Alive. The book still sells thousands of copies each year.

26. Mawi Asgedom self-published his memoir, Of Beetles and Angels, which told the story of his journey from war-torn Ethiopia at age three to a refugee camp in Sudan, a childhood on welfare in an American suburb, and eventual triumph as a Harvard graduate, where he gave the commencement address in 1999. In 2001, he sold rights to that book and another nonfiction book (featuring advice for teenagers drawn from his motivational speeches), to Little, Brown for six figures.

27. Stephanie Dircks Ashcraft never expected to sell thousands of copies of the book of recipes that she and her husband once assembled by hand in their small living room in Utah. She created the first copy of 101 Things to Do with a Cake Mix as a college class project, then a few months later began teaching a cooking class based on the book at a local supermarket. Her students pleaded with her to put all the recipes together in a book, which led to her first print run and several subsequent reprintings.

Over 7000 copies of Stephanie's self-published version sold locally in Utah, the Intermountain West, and on the web. In August 2002, Gibbs-Smith published a new edition of the book and gave it national distribution. By mid-October 2002, the book had hit #9 on the New York Times paperback advice bestseller list.

28. Tami Oldham Ashcraft former her own publishing company, Bright Works Publishing, to self-publish her story of surviving Hurricane Raymond out in the Pacific Ocean (Red Sky in Mourning). After selling more than 8,000 copies of her edition, a literary agent discovered the book while biking on the San Juan Islands. Several months later, the agent sold the reprint rights to Hyperion for half a million dollars.

29. Best-selling Canadian author Margaret Atwood self-published her first volume of poetry Double Persephone in 1961, the year she graduated from college. The print run was only 200 copies. Atwood has gone on to become a best-selling novelist and short story writer.

30. In the fall of 2004, Joe Babcock, winner of the Writer's Digest International Self-Published book award, sold rights to his novel The Tragedy of Miss Geneva Flowers to Carroll & Graf with the help of agent Michael Mancilla of Greystone Literary Agency.

31. After promoting his self-published book, The Truth about Relationships, on more than 800 radio shows, Dr. Greg Baer and his agent Wendy Sherman sold rights to Gotham for its debut list where the book was published as Real Love.

32. A scrap booking enthusiast, Wendy Bagley self-published a collection of funny essays on the subject called Scraps. Later with the help of literary agent Jenny Bent of Trident Media Group, she sold the reprint rights to Hyperion for six figures.

33. After selling 7,000 copies of her self-published first novel A Little Piece of Sky, Nicole Bailey-Williams sold reprint

rights to Harlem Moon, the African-American imprint of Bantam Doubleday Dell.

34. African-American author Michael Baisden has been self-publishing his own hardcover novels and then selling paperback reprint rights to Simon & Schuster's Touchstone imprint. The trade paperback edition of his novel The Maintenance Man hit the USA Today bestseller list.

35. In 1983, Phyllis Balch self-published her first book Nutritional Outline for the Professional and the Wise Man with her then-husband James F. Balch. That book was later titled Prescription for Nutritional Healing when it was picked up by Avery in 1990.

36. Cheryl and Peter Barnes started up Vacation Spot Books by self-publishing Peter's children's book, Nat, Nat, the Nantucket Cat, in 1992. They sold the first edition of 5,000 copies within a year and continue to sell about 5,000 copies every year since that time.

   In 2001, Cheryl met Mattie J.T. Stepanek, a child poet suffering from a rare form of muscular dystrophy, while working as a volunteer at Washington, D.C.'s Children's Hospital. Inspired by his spirit and poems, she went on to publish several collections of his poems. Heartsongs and Journey Through Heartsongs both made it to the New York Times bestseller list after Mattie appeared on Oprah.

37. John Bartlett financed and published the first three editions of Familiar Quotations, the bestselling quote book on the market.

38. L. Frank Baum self-published at least some of the books in the Wizard of Oz series.

39. Jonathan Bayliss, a mainstay of Gloucester, Massachusett's literary inner circle since the 1950's,

began self-publishing three innovative novels in his Gloucesterman series starting in 1992. In 1999, the Boston Globe called him "one of the great self-published authors of our time."

40. John Bear self-published Bears' Guide to Earning Degrees by Distance Learning in 1972 and sold more than 200,000 copies by direct mail before he sold rights to Ten Speed Press in 1983.

41. In the spring of 2004, attorney Philip Beard was about to write a check for the printer to self-publish his novel Dear Zoe when Clare Ferraro, president of Viking Press, called to make an offer on his book.

    Beard's bookseller friend, John Towle of Aspinwall Bookstore, loved his book and had recommended it to a visiting sales rep, John Gobble of Penguin. Taking a chance on a self-published title, Gobble read the book and loved it. He, in turn, recommended the novel to Ferraro, who promptly bought the book.

42. In 1993, Barry Beckham wrote and published the first Black Student's Guide to Colleges. In addition, he developed the Black Student's Guide to Scholarships. These books and others helped him to create the Beckham Publications Group.

43. Impressionist artist Guy Begin, the Painter of Perfumes, created his own first break by self-publishing his artwork as lithographs, serigraphs, and note cards. He now licenses his artwork to six companies.

44. In 1985, Paula Begoun self-published her first book, Blue Eye Shadow Should Be Illegal (now called The Beauty Bible), a how-to book on using the right cosmetics. She followed the success of her first book by writing and publishing a second book called Don't Go to the Cosmetics Counter Without Me.

A few years later, she also published another follow-up called Don't Go Shopping for Hair Care Products Without Me. All told, these three beauty books have sold more than two million copies in the past thirteen years.

45. In 1928, Peter Beilenson began publishing books from the Peter Pauper Press using a foot-treadle press in his father's basement to publish books "at prices even a pauper could afford." For more than 75 years, the press has continued as a family business.

46. Pierre Bennu sold rights to his self-published book Bullsh**t or Fertilizer to Andrews McMeel. Rights have also been sold to digicube and Japan.

47. Todd Bermont is author and self-publisher of 10 Insider Secrets to Job Hunting Success and 10 Insider Secrets Career Transition Workshop.

48. In 2000, author ReShonda Tate Billingsley had a story to tell and sent out a flood of query letters trying to interest agents in her novel, My Brother's Keeper. "I tried to go the traditional route and sent out letters to agents," she said. That didn't work. So she decided to self-publish.

   Within a year, she and her friends had sold 15,000 copies and one of the larger publishers, Simon & Schuster, came calling. Now she has a contract with them to publish nine more books in the next two years.

49. Ken Blanchard and Spencer Johnson originally self-published The One-Minute Manager so they could sell the book for $15.00 at a time when all the experts were telling them that they'd never sell the book for such a high price.

   In a three month time, they sold over 20,000 copies in the San Diego area alone — and then sold the reprint rights to William Morrow. The One-Minute Manager has sold more than 12 million copies since 1982 and been published in 25+ languages.

50. 31-year-old British author Marc Blaney self-published Two Kinds of Silence to the sound of silence. So he decided to submit his book for the Somerset Maugham award (for young authors) so he could tell booksellers that his book had been entered for the award. Well, he won. He was flabbergasted: "I didn't expect in a million years to win."

51. In 2000, after getting 70 rejections for his comic novel, screenwriter John Blumenthal self-published a trade paperback of What's Wrong with Dorfman?, which was selected by January magazine as one of the 50 best books of 2000. He went on to get more major reviews and finally sold the book to St. Martin's Press for a nice sum of money.

52. In the 1970's, American poet Robert Bly self-published many of his poetry books and translations through his own publishing company.

53. Richard N. Bolles originally self-published What Color Is Your Parachute as a small typed guide for Episcopal priests who needed to readjust after leaving the priesthood. Later he sold the rights to Ten Speed Press. The book has now spent 288 weeks on the New York Times bestseller list and returns to other bestseller lists (such as Business Week's) each year when a new edition comes out.

54. Since 1973, Australian dietician Allan Borushek has sold more than 11 million copies of his self-published calorie counter books and other products in the U.S. and Australia. About 8 million copies were sold in Australia, which is an amazing feat considering that Australia has a population equivalent to Texas.

55. Former Major League baseball pitcher and best-selling author Jim Bouton decided to self-publish Foul Ball through his Bulldog Press in 2003. The book, an account

of his efforts to preserve the oldest minor-league ballpark in the U.S. (at Pittsfield, Massachusetts), was originally sold to Public Affairs but after an editorial dispute, Bouton decided to self-publish.

56. Ruby Ann Boxcar, Trailer Park newspaper columnist and web site host, self-published her first book, Ruby Ann's Down Home Trailer Park Cookbook, via POD through iUniverse.com. The rights were quickly snapped up Kensington/Citadel Press which has since gone on to publish Ruby Ann's holiday cookbook. Ruby Ann is known as the Dame Edna of the double-wide world. She is a crowd pleaser. At regional book shows, she autographs and kisses every book before handing them over to booksellers.

57. Stewart Brand self-published the first editions of The Whole Earth Catalog before selling the rights to a larger publisher. The Catalog, famous for widely disseminating the first photograph of the earth from space, was the bible of the back to the land movement. More than one edition of the Catalog hit the New York Times bestseller list.

58. Hilery Bradt self-published her first award-winning guidebook and now publishes a growing list of travel guides by other writers under her imprint, Bradt Travel Guides.

59. Engineer Marshall Brain began by publishing his work as a hobby on his web site http://www.HowStuffWorks.com. This site features colorful easily understood illustrations and simple explanations to describe how things work, from how a black hole works to an expresso machine to plasma TV to Christmas lights.

The site has grown to a business with more than 20 staff, numerous spin-offs, and $20 million in annual revenue. Two volumes of How Stuff Works have been published by John Wiley.

60. Jeff Brauer started On Your Own Books in the basement of his parent's house. He had begun working on his first book, Sexy New York (a Zagat-like guide to the kinky places in New York) while still in law school. In 2002, while still running his Brooklyn-based publishing company, Brauer also ran for Congress from a district on the east side of Manhattan.

61. David Brody self-published his book Unlawful Deeds via iUniverse's print-on-demand program. He sold almost 3,000 copies in his home area of Boston, Massachusetts while doing 26 bookstore appearances. At one point, his book hit #8 on the Boston Globe bestseller list. His book is probably the first print-on-demand book to hit a bestseller list.

62. Amanda Brown used First Books to publish her first novel Legally Blonde as a print-on-demand book. Her self-published book was made into a movie starring Reese Witherspoon. A year and a half after the movie was made, Plume published her book, with an additional chapter on what's next for Elle Woods.

63. H. Jackson Brown originally self-published his Life's Little Instruction Book. Soon thereafter, the book was bought by Rutledge Hill, a local publisher, who went on to sell more than 5 million copies. The book made the bestseller lists in both hardcover and softcover and continues to be a great seller around graduation time every year.

64. English poet Elizabeth Barrett Browning, author of Sonnets from the Portuguese, paid for the publication of her first book.

65. After being dissatisfied with the results of regular publishers, Dorothy Bryant and her husband Bob established Ata Books to self-publish her next four novels, all of which didn't fit the acceptable mold of current

publishers. Here's what Pat Holt of Holt Uncensored has said about Bryant:

"With Ella Price's Journal, for example, Bryant anticipated the movement of middle-aged women returning to college in droves; The Kin of Ata was the first of many spiritual-mentor novels by such writers as Carlos Castaneda, Lynn Andrews, Dan Millman and others; with Prisoners.

Bryant foresaw the trend by liberals such as Norman Mailer of sponsoring the release of convicts they knew nothing about, and didn't want to; her novel, The Test, was among the first books to recognize the dilemma of middle-aged baby boomers caring for both their own kids and their own aging parents; A Day in San Francisco was her portentous 1983 novel about a mother's concern over her gay son and what Dorothy calls 'a liberation movement gone astray' (only a year before gay bowel syndrome was recognized as a disease called AIDS)."

66. Nick Bunick, an Oregon businessman, self-published The Messengers by Julia Ingram and G.W. Hardin. This nonfiction book tells the true story of Bunick and his experiences with angels and reincarnation. Self-publishing the book at the end of 1996, Bunick spent $160,000 promoting it. Through his marketing efforts, more than 20,000 copies were sold in a few short months in the Portland and Seattle areas alone. A few months later, he sold the rights to that book and a sequel for $1,000,000 to Pocket Books. Did his efforts pay off? You do the math.

67. Edgar Rice Burroughs, author of the Tarzan books, self-published some of his books.

68. William Byham self-published the best-selling business book, Zapp: The Lightning of Empowerment. At the time of this writing, this business book has sold more than 2.5

million copies in self-published and Crown Publishing editions.

69. In 1975, Ernest Callenbach self-published his counterculture classic Ecotopia. The book was reprinted by Bantam in 1977.

70. Before selling rights to Putnam, Julia Cameron self-published her best-selling The Artist's Way. The book has sold more than a million copies now.

71. Professional gambler Avery Cardoza built a publishing empire writing and publishing gambling advice books. In 2003, he took it a step further by publishing a new magazine, Avery Cardoza's Player, for the amateur gambler.

72. Richard Carlson, author of the best-selling Don't Sweat the Small Stuff series, began his book career by self-publishing The Business of Bodywork.

73. Ricki Carroll and her then-husband Robert self-published Cheesemaking Made Easy in 1982, four years after starting the New England Cheesemaking Supply Company. Later they sold the rights to Storey Publications. That first book sold more than 100,000 copies. In 2002, Ricki brought out a new edition with Storey Publications called Home Cheese Making.

74. Cindy Cashman, with her then partner Alan Garner, self-published Everything Men Know about Women (using the pseudonym of Dr. Alan Francis) and sold more than half a million copies of the blank book before selling rights to Andrews-McMeel. The book has now sold more than 1.5 million copies.

75. In 1977, student teacher John Cassidy joined with two college pals to self-publish Juggling for the Complete Klutz as a stapled little book, which had come out of a mimeographed high school lesson plan. The book went on

to sell more than 2.5 million copies and led to the establishment of Klutz Press, which has published fifty books.

76. Novelist Willa Cather paid for the publication of her first book. Her novel, One of Ours, won the Pulitzer Prize.

77. When Dave Chilton self-published The Wealthy Barber in 1989, he took a long-term view to building the book. He dedicated himself to doing hundreds of interviews during that first year. By 1990, his book was selling ten to fifteen thousand copies a month. By 1991, his book had made the Canadian bestseller list. By 1996, it was still on the Canadian bestseller lists. With more than a million copies sold (in a country of 29 million!), his book is the best-selling book in Canadian history, excluding the Bible.

78. Deepak Chopra vanity published his first book and then sold the rights to Crown Publishing. The book went on to become the first of many New York Times bestsellers for this author.

79. British journalist Stephen Clarke originally self-published in France his travel adventures, A Year in the Merde. Since publishing the book, he and his agent Susanna Lea of Susanna Lea Associates have sold U.S. rights to Bloomsbury, for publication in spring 2005, as well as French rights to Laffont, Australian rights to Random House, and UK rights to Transworld.

80. Will Clarke self-published his first novel, Lord Vishnu's Love Handles. It got the attention of a film writer, Grant Morris, who persuaded Will to give him a free option. The movie is now getting made at Paramount, and the book is being published by Simon and Schuster (with the help of agent Jenny Bent of Trident Media Group), as is Will's second novel, also self-published, The Worthy.

81. With the help of his agent Jimmy Vines, Dr. Will Clower

sold his self-published book The Fat Fallacy to Crown.

82. After selling over 20,000 copies of his self-published novel Before I Let Go in less than four months (primarily via independent bookstores on the East Coast), Darren Coleman with the help of agent Jimmy Vines sold rights to that novel as well as another to Amistad/Harper.

83. After self-publishing three chick lit crime novels, Jennifer Colt sold rights to all three novels (The Butcher of Beverly Hills, The Mangler of Malibu Canyon, and The Vampire of Venice Beach) to Broadway Books with the help of agent Jenny Bent of Trident Media Group.

84. Best-selling novelist Pat Conroy self-published his first book, The Boo. He spent thousands on printing and promoting the book. Now, of course, his advances run much, much higher. His best-selling books include The Prince of Tides, The Great Santini, The Lords of Discipline, Beach Music, My Losing Season, and The Water Is Wide.

85. Wade Cook, through his various companies, has self-published many of his best-selling books, including Stock Market Miracles and Wall Street Money Machine (500,000 copies).

86. Nick Corcodilos self-published Ask the Headhunter. For the first two years he made a profit in the mid-six figures. In the third year a major publisher offered him a high five-figures advance and he sold the rights.

87. Laura Corn self-published 101 Nights of Grrreat Sex and several other books. She sold 100,000 copies of 237 Intimate Questions Every Woman Should Ask a Man from the trunk of her car. Total sales for 101 Nights was 525,000 copies as of March 1999.

88. Steve Crist, owner of The Daily Racing Form, published his own book under DRF Books his memoir, Myself:

Adventures of a Horse-player and Publisher.

89. American poet e.e. cummings self-published No Thanks, a volume of poetry financed by his mother. On the half-title page, he listed the thirteen publishers who had rejected the book, which became one of his classics.

90. Norman F. Dacey self-published the bestseller, How to Avoid Probate.

91. In 2001, Lisa Daily self-published Stop Getting Dumped. With the help of publicist Sherri Rosen, she got so much publicity for the book that she was able to sell the rights to Penguin for a very nice sum.

92. Diana Dalsass, author of five cookbooks published by NAL, Norton and Contemporary, self-published The Butterscotch Lover's Cookbook, under her Buttercup Press imprint so she'd have more control over its design.

93. In 1973, Bill Dalton self-published A Traveler's Notes: Indonesia. By the time he sold the company he had founded, Moon Publications, it had published almost 100 titles and was the largest American publisher of guidebooks for independent travelers.

94. Half African-American, half-Blackfoot Jamise L. Dames sold more than 30,000 copies of her first novel Mamma's Baby, Daddy's Maybe. The novel even made the Essence bestseller list.

95. Dennis Damp founded Brookhaven Press to self-publish The Book of Government Jobs, which has now been through 8 editions.

96. After Craig Danner made a big impression at regional trade shows in the Pacific Northwest and northern California, booksellers began ordering his self-published novel Himalayan Dhaba. The book was then named as a Book Sense 76 pick. In a heated auction, Dutton won the

right to republish the book as a hardcover for a high-altitude six-figures.

97. Renny Darling of Royal House Publishing sold more than a half million copies her first cookbook, The Joy of Eating.

98. In 1933, Charles Darrow invented the game of Monopoly. Parker Brothers had originally rejected the game because of "52 design flaws," so Darrow produced the game himself and quickly sold 5,000 games to a Philadelphia department store. The rest is history. Parker Brothers changed their minds and took on the production and marketing of the game. More than 200 million copies of Monopoly have been sold thus far.

99. Mary Janice Davidson began by publishing her romance novels as e-books at www.ellorascave.com, a web site featuring saucy romantic fantasies. A friend of hers brought her novels to the attention of Cindy Hwang, an editor at Berkley, who liked one of them enough (Undead and Unwed) to offer a three-book deal.

100. Max Davis originally self-published his book, Never Stick Your Tongue Out at Momma, then sold the rights to Bantam Doubleday Dell. As a self-promoter, he sold more copies of the BDD edition than the publisher did. He sold the rights to his next book to Penguin Putnam.

101. In 1998, Verna Burger Davis self-published her memoirs, My Chosen Trails, at the age of 96. Her granddaughter, Amy Martin, and son, Jim Davis, with financing by Verna, set up the publishing company, Deep Creek Press. Verna did all of the writing about her life through the 20th century. The first printing sold over 2,000 copies and, in 2003, she was preparing to go to a second printing with an additional chapter, detailing the ensuing five years and the changes that being an author brought in her life.

102. Afrikadzata Deku has self-published 40 books, including Sacred Verses for My Afrikan Queens, The Power of Afrikan-Centricity, and The Afrikan Truth.

103. When Kathleen Dexter self-published her fairy tale love story, Fifth Life of the Catwoman, it was chosen as a BookSense 76 pick. The book was then sold to Berkley where it once more became a BookSense 76 pick.

104. Don Dible originally self-published the New York Times best-selling book, Up Your Own Organization.

105. In 1978, train buff Chuck Ditlefsen self-published his first calendar, Those Magnificent Trains. Since then, he has built his company, Cedco Publishing, into one of the fastest-growing companies in America (it made the Inc. 500 list in 1998).

106. Ben Dominitz self-published several books, one on free travel (Travel Free) and another on romance, before completely establishing Prima Publishing, one of the largest of the independent small publishers. In less than fifteen years, he built a company that had published well over 1,500 titles, had more than 140 employees, and competed with New York publishers on an equal standing. Prima was sold to Random House in 2001.

107. Laura Doyle originally self-published The Surrendered Wife. Once it became the best-selling book in Washington State, she sold reprint rights to Simon & Schuster. The book went on to become a New York Times bestseller.

108. After Canadian writer Oriah Mountain Dreamer's prose poem The Invitation appeared on dozens of web sites, agent Joe Durepos helped her to sell the rights to the poem in book form to Harper SanFrancisco in 1999, where it became a bestseller and has been translated into more than 15 languages around the world. She self-published a small chapbook of poetry, Dreams of Desire, in 1995.

109. American civil rights leader William E.B. Du Bois, co-founder of the NAACP, self-published The Moon in 1906. He went on to edit the Crisis journal from 1910 to 1932 as well as write other books, including Color and Democracy, that promoted the concerns of African-Americans.

110. Doug DuBosque started Peel Productions to publish and promote his drawing books for kids, including Draw 3-D, Draw Cars, Draw Ocean Animals, Draw Rainforest Animals, Draw Desert Animals, Draw Grassland Animals, Draw Insects, Draw Dinosaurs, and Learn To Draw Now. Since then he has sold more than 6 million copies of the 60 tiles he has published, both his own books and those of other artists.

111. In a little over two years, author Laura Duksta and illustrator Karen Keesler sold 130,000 copies of their first book, I Love You More. Available now in 46 states, the book sells best through eclectic gift shops, art galleries, children's boutiques, and great independent bookstores.

112. French novelist Alexandre Dumas, author of such swashbuckling romances as The Three Musketeers and The Count of Monte Cristo, self-published some of his first books.

113. Paul Laurence Dunbar, the first African-American poet to achieve national prominence, published his first poetry collection at the age of 21 after being invited to read his poetry at the 1893 World's Fair. Before that he had published an African-American newsletter, the Dayton Tattler, with the help of his classmates Wilbur and Orville Wright. He went on to publish many more collections of poetry, several novels, librettos, and scripts. He is known as the poet laureate of African Americans.

114. In 1989, Cyndi Duncan and Georgie Patrick began C & G Publishing by self-publishing Colorado Cookie Collection, a collection of favorite recipes collected over

ten years from cookie exchanges held in their homes. During their years of publishing, they have won eight Evvy Awards (from the Colorado Independent Publishers Association) and a Benjamin Franklin award for Nothin' But Muffins.

115. Hale Dwoskin and Lester Levenson sold more than 20,000 copies of their self-published book, Happiness Is Free: And It's Easier Than You Think, via their web site and various online bookstores. To promote the book, Dwoskin began by emailing thousands of his former students at Sedona Training Associates. Their response was to propel the book to the top of the list at Amazon.com.

116. With the help of six friends, Betty J. Eadie self-published Embraced by the Light, which went on to become a New York Times bestseller (on the list for two years as a hardcover and paperback).

117. Mary Baker Eddy, founder of The First Church of Christ, Scientists, originally self-published her book, Science and Health with Key to the Scriptures, in 1875. That book is now published in 17 languages and has sold more than ten million copies worldwide. Eddy also founded her own publishing company which today publishes weekly and monthly magazines as well as the Pulitzer Prize award-winning daily newspaper, The Christian Science Monitor (founded in 1908).

118. Bob Easter wrote and published two books on buying and selling homes. He has sold thousands of copies via his web site at http://www.easterhome.com.

119. With the help of agent Anna Ghosh, India Edghill sold the rights to her self-published novel Queenmaker to St. Martin's which offered her a big advance and full-page ads in the New York Times Book Review.

120. In 2002, best-selling author Dave Eggers (A Heartbreaking Work of Staggering Genius) published his first novel through his own publishing company, McSweeney's.

121. Arlene Eisenberg self-published What to Do When You're Expecting before Workman went on to republish it and sell 8 million copies (and counting) plus millions more copies of other titles in the series.

122. Nobel Prize-winning poet T.S. Eliot, author of The Love Song of J. Alfred Prufrock and The Waste Land, paid for the publication of his first book.

123. In 2002, best-selling author Dave Eggers (A Heartbreaking Work of Staggering Genius) published his first novel through his own publishing company, McSweeney's. He sold 10,000 copies as a limited edition through his web site mcsweeneys.net. Books published by McSweeney's are printed in Iceland.

124. Paulette Ensign's success in selling 500,000 booklets (110 Ideas for Organizing Your Business Life without Advertising) shows you can have success in self publishing without needing to write a full length book. Her website is www.tipsbooklets.com.

125. John Erickson founded Maverick Books to self-publish the first book in his Hank the Cowdog series in 1982. To make sales, he loaded his pickup with copies and sold them at cattle auctions, rodeos, schools, Rotary meetings, and anywhere else he could find a crowd. He later sold the series to Texas Monthly Press, which was later bought by Gulf Publishing.

126. Steve Eunpu has sold more than 650,000 copies of The 20 Gram Diet book.

127. Due to demand from many friends, Richard Paul Evans self-published 8,000 copies of his little holiday story, The

Christmas Box, in August 1993. That fall he sold many thousands of copies in the Salt Lake City area alone. When the major publishers became interested in the book, dozens of them participated in a two-day auction. Simon & Schuster came out the winner. They only had to pay Evans a $4.2 million advance (which included the rights to a prequel as well). He retained the rights to his softcover edition. The next year, both editions ended up on the bestseller lists. The book has sold more than 7 million copies in 17 different languages.

128. When Jim Everroad lost his job as a high school athletic coach, he decided to become a sportswriter. The first job he tackled was to write an article describing the exercises he had developed to tighten his pot belly. After selling the article to a newspaper, he expanded it into a full book called How to Flatten Your Stomach and printed a first edition of 3,000 copies. Later the book was discovered by Price/Stern/Sloan who published a national edition of the book, which became a bestseller. The book has since sold over 2 million copies.

129. Twenty-five years ago, Helen Exley self-published the first of her many illustrated quote gift books. Since 1976, Exley Publications has sold more than 41 million copies of her gift books.

130. New Harbinger's president, Patrick Fanning, conceived of founding the company over a box lunch with publisher Matthew McKay. The first book they published, The Relaxation & Stress Reduction Workbook, was one they co-authored. It has now sold over 450,000 copies. New Harbinger grew slowly, with McKay and Fanning writing many titles themselves.

131. In 1951, Howard Fast couldn't find a publisher for his novel Spartacus because he was a member of the Communist Party and therefore blacklisted at that time.

So he published the book himself. It became a bestseller and went on to be made into an incredible movie. In 1956, Fast broke with the Communist Party after revelations of Stalin-era atrocities.

132. Father and son team Jim and Charles Fay, along with Foster Cline, formed the Love and Logic Institute to self-publish an entire line of self-help parenting books, including Love and Logic Magic for Early Childhood, Grandparenting with Love and Logic, Oh Great! What Do I Do Now?, Toddlers and Pre-Schoolers: Love and Logic Parenting for Early Childhood, Hormones & Wheels, Developing Character in Teens, Parenting Teens with Love and Logic, Trouble-Free Teens, and more.

133. In 1953, Lawrence Ferlinghetti founded City Lights Bookstore. Soon thereafter, he self-published Pictures of the Gone World, his classic book of poems, as the first of many books published by City Lights Books, including such books as Allan Ginsberg's Howl and Other Poems. About 30 years later, he became the first living writer to have a San Francisco street named after him.

134. Nature and environmental photographer John Fielder founded Westcliffe Publishers, which has published 31 of his exhibit format books and guide books, including John Fielder's Best of Colorado and Colorado 1870 - 2000 (Colorado's best-selling book ever).

135. Canadian lawyers Barry Fish and Les Kotzer sold more than 15,000 copies of their self-published book on wills and estates, The Family Fight: Planning to Avoid It, within the first nine months of publication. Most of those orders were generated via mail order from publicity in publications like the Wall Street Journal and New York Times.

136. Here's a little self starter proof that books by writing groups do sell. For example, Wednesday Writers: Ten

Years of Writing Women's Lives, edited by Elizabeth Fishel and Terri Hinte, hit #7 on the San Francisco Chronicle's bestseller list, right behind Laura Hillenbrand's *Seabiscuit*.

137. Bill Fisher began his publishing career by self-publishing performance car manuals in 1947. Later, in 1963, he and his wife Helen founded HP (horse power) Books, which they sold to Knight-Ridder in 1979. Eight years later, they founded another company, Fisher Books.

138. British poet and translator Edward Fitzgerald paid to have the first copies of his translation of The Rubaiyat of Omar Khayyam published in 1859. The book has sold millions of copies since its first publication.

139. E. Randall Floyd founded Harbor House in 1998 to self-publish his Civil War novel Deep in the Heart, which has since sold 100,000 copies. The company now publishes five to ten titles per year. In 2003, Harbor House was named one of the 15 small publisher standouts by Publishers Weekly.

140. In hopes of getting another bestseller like those from the Delaney sisters, Warner Books paid 98-year-old Jessie Lee Brown Foveaux more than $1 million for the rights to her self-published reminiscences, Any Given Day. The book had been only a modest self-published success.

141. Les and Sue Fox self-published The Beanie Baby Handbook in 1997. By July of 1998, they had gone back to press eight more times for an in-print total of 3 million copies while the book established itself in the #2 spot on the New York Times bestseller list (under advice, how-to, and miscellaneous). Later in 1998, they published the Beanie Baby Cookbook.

142. Business consultant Tom Peters self-published In Search of Excellence and sold more than 25,000 copies

directly to consumers in the first year. He then sold the rights to Warner, whose edition has gone on to sell more than 10 million copies.

143. Jo Petty paid a vanity press to publish the first printing of Apples of Gold. A few years later, in 1965, she sold the rights to C.R. Gibson Company, a gift and stationery company. In the next 20 years, 3.7 million copies were sold.

144. At the age of 26, Ben Franklin, using the pen name of Richard Saunders, self-published his Poor Richard's Almanack in 1732 and continued to produce the almanac for another 26 years. Many of his famous sayings came from the Almanack. Because of the success of his printing and publishing business, Franklin was able to retire at the age of 42. He became one of the world's greatest scientists and inventors (inventing bifocals, the Franklin stove, and the lightning rod). He ended his life as a statesman and one of the key founders of the United States of America as a signer of the Declaration of Independence.

145. Criswell Freemen has compiled and self-published more than 70 books of quotations, including such titles as The Book of Stock Car Wisdom, The Fisherman's Book of Wisdom, The Wisdom of Women's Golf as well as Friends Are Forever, Fathers Are Forever, Mothers Are Forever, etc. He published his first three quote books in 1994: The Book of Country Music Wisdom, Wisdom Made in America, and The Book of Southern Wisdom. Since then, he has sold more than 6 million copies of these gift books.

146. In 2002, former journalist Mister Mann Frisby sold over 10,000 copies of his self-published urban thriller Blinking Red Light in Philadelphia alone. Then with the help of Los Bravos Management, he sold reprint rights to Riverhead for that book as well as a second novel.

147. In 1985, Ron Fry began Career Press by publishing several career directories that he edited. He went on to publish his classic 101 Great Answers to the Toughest Interview Questions and his How to Study program (a series of six books that have sold more than 2 million copies).

148. Joanne Watson originally self-published How to Help Your Husband Make More Money, So You Can Be a Stay-at-Home Mom and then sold the rights to Warner Books.

149. Aliske Webb self-published her novel, Twelve Golden Threads: Lessons for Successful Living from Grama's Quilt, and went on a two-and-a-half year tour of quilt shows to sell the book. Soon thereafter, HarperCollins signed her to a four-book contract for a healthy sum. Now as publisher of Book Mice (http://www.bookmice.com/aliskewebb.htm), she is helping other authors to get their books out to the public.

150. Michael Webb began by publishing a small 8-page newsletter of romantic tips and ideas. From that small beginning, his relationship business has grown to include six best-selling books on romance, including The Romantic's Guide: Hundreds of Creative Tips for a Lifetime of Love.

Now that you have been properly inspired, go out and publish your own book or books. Make it different, make it count and make it yours.

Appendix III

INDEPENDENT PUBLISHERS DIRECTORY

1. Aegis Publishing Group, Robert Mastin, President, 796 Aquidneck Avenue, Middletown RI 02840; 401-849-4200; 800-828-6961; Fax: 401-849-4231. Email: aegis@aegisbooks.com. Specialty: telecommunications books.

2. Allworth Press, Tad Crawford, Publisher, 10 East 23rd Street #210, New York NY 10010; 212-777-8395; 800-491-2808; Fax: 212-777-8261. Email: pub@allworth.com. Specialty: arts and writing.

3. Amber-Allen, Janet Mills, Editor and Publisher, P O Box 6657, San Rafael CA 94903; 415-499-4657; 800-624-8855; Fax: 415-499-3174. Email: janet@amberallen.com. Specialty: new age.

4. American Historic Inns, Deborah Sakach, Publisher, P O Box 669, Dana Point CA 92629; 714-499-8070; Fax: 714-499-4022. Email: ahii@ix.netcom.com.

5. Amherst Media, Craig Alesse, Publisher, 155 Rano Street #300, Buffalo NY 14207; 716-874-4450; Fax: 716-874-4508. A publisher of photography, video, imaging, and astronomy books and videos.

6. Applewood Press, Phil Zuckerman, Publisher, 128 The Great Road, P O Box 365, Bedford MA 01730; 781-271-0055; Fax: 781-271-0056. Founded in 1976, they specialize in reprinting old titles on American history, popular culture, and nostalgia. They have 250 books in print.

7. Atlantic Publishing Company, Robbe Lankford, 1405 SW 6th Avenue, Ocala FL 34474; 352-622-1825; Fax: 352-622-

1875. Email: rlankford@atlantic-pub.com. Publisher of real estate guides and other business guides.

8. August House, Ted and Liz Parkhurst, Publishers, P O Box 3223, Little Rock AR 72203; 501-372-5450; 800-284-8784. Fax: 501-372-5579. Email: ahinfo@augusthouse.com. Founded in 1980. Specialties: storytelling, folklore, regional and multicultural titles.

9. Avalon Publishing Group, Charlie Winton, President, 245 West 17th Street, 11th Floor, New York NY 10011-5300; 212-981-9919 or 646-375-2570; Fax: 646-375-2571. Avalon Travel Publishing, Seal Press, Shoemaker & Hoard Publishers, 1400 65th Street #250, Emeryville CA 94608; 510-595-3664; Fax: 510-595-4228. This company grew out of Publishers Group West, a distributor, as PGW began acquiring some of the companies it distributed. Now independent, Avalon consists of a number of smaller publishers, including Avalon Travel Publishing (Moon Publications, Foghorn Press), Carroll & Graf, Thunder's Mouth, Nation Books, Seal Press, Shoemaker & Hoard Publishers, and Marlowe & Co.

10. Bard Press, Ray Bard, Editor, 5275 McCormick Mountain Drive, Austin TX 78734; 512-266-2112; Fax: 512-266-2749. Email: ray@bardpress.com. Specialty: business books.

11. Barefoot Books, Tessa Strickland & Nancy Traversy, 2067 Massachusetts Avenue, Cambridge MA 02140; 617-576-0660; 866-417-2369; Fax: 617-576-0049. Email: ussales@barefoot-books.com. U.S. office; main office in the U.K. Specializes in children's story books.

12. Berrett-Koehler Publishers, Steven Piersanti, Publisher, 235 Montgomery Street #650, San Francisco CA 94104; 415-288-0260; 800-929-2929; Fax: 415-362-2512. Email: bkpub@aol.com. Web: http://www.bkconnection.com. Founded in 1992, they are spearheading the Consortium

for Business Literacy to encourage the reading of books by business leaders, managers, and workers. Specialties: business, human resources, career development, management.

13. Bess Press, Buddy Bess, Publisher, 3565 Harding Avenue, Honolulu HI 96816; 808-734-7159; 800-910-2377; Fax: 808-732-3627. Email: kelly@besspress.com. Since 1979. Specializes in Hawaii and the Pacific.

Ready to get those books stacked in your garage into the hands of even MORE readers? Earma has harnessed the power of internet promotion into one place to set your book ablaze with new sales. Get the ebook Ten Easy Ways to Market Your Book Online with software bonuses that help you promote your book to a new market - the WORLD. Visit here http://bookmarketinghelp.com for details.

14. Black Classic Press, W. Paul Coates, Publisher, P O Box 13414, Baltimore MD 21203; 410-358-0980; Fax: 410-358-0987. Email: BCP@charm.net. Specialty: Black books.

15. John F. Blair Publisher, Carolyn Sakowski, President, 1406 Plaza Drive, Winston-Salem NC 27103; 336-768-1374; 800-222-9796; Fax: 336-768-9194. Email: sakowski@blairpub.com. Founded in 1954, this independent family-owned company publishes about 20 titles per year. Specialties: fiction, regional.

16. Blue Pearl Press, Christopher Hartman, President, 8950 W Olympic Boulevard #416, Beverly Hills CA 90211; 888-266-5708. Specialties: health, spirituality, fiction, controversial books.

17. Bonus Books. Specialties: business, fund-raising, sports, media.

18. Book Peddlers, Vicki Lansky, Publisher, 15245 Minnetonka Boulevard, Minnetonka MN 55345-1510; 612-912-0036; 800-255-3379; Fax: 612-912-0105. Email: dearvicki@aol.com. Web: http://www.practicalparenting.com. Specialty: parenting books, household hints, and Christmas titles.

19. Bramble Books, Larry K. Bramble, Publisher, 8600 Boulevard East #5C, North Bergen NJ 07047; 201-861-7730; Fax: 508-734-2178. Email: info@bramblebooks.com.

20. Brick Tower Press, John T Colby Jr., Publisher, 1230 Park Avenue, New York NY 10128; 212-427-7139. Email: bricktower@aol.com. Primary specialties: cooking and maritime.

21. Bridge Works, Warren Phillips, Publisher; Barbara Phillips, Editorial Director, P O Box 1798, Bridgehampton NY 11932; 516-537-3418; Fax: 516-537-5092. Specialties: fiction.

22. The Brookfield Reader,137 Peyton Road, Sterling VA 20165-5605; 888-389-2741; Fax: 703-430-7315. Email: info@brookfieldreader.com. The 1999 Small Press Publisher of the Year publishes wonderful children's books.

23. Burford Books, Peter Burford, Publisher, 32 Morris Avenue, Springfield NJ 07081; 973-258-0960; Fax: 973-258-0113. Email: info@burfordbooks.com. Specialties: golf, war histories and memoirs, fly fishing, cookbooks.

24. Butterfly Press, Varn and Earma Brown, Publishers, P.O. 180141, Dallas, TX 75218; 877-846-9908; Fax: 877-846-9908. Email: info@butterflypress.net. Specialties: Writing Helps; Christian Religious/Inspirational Non-Fiction; Family Heritage; Religious Women Non-Fiction.

25. Camino Books, Edward Jutkowitz, Publisher; Carol Hupping, Editor, P O Box 59026, Philadelphia PA 19102;

215-413-1917; Fax: 215-413-3255. Email: camino@caminobooks.com. Founded in 1987, Camino publishes books of regional interest to people in the mid-Atlantic states. Specialties: cooking, gardening, travel, regional history, biographies, health. They publish six to ten books a year.

26. Career Press, Ron Fry, Publisher, 3 Tice Road, P O Box 687, Franklin Lakes NJ 07417; 201-848-0310; 800-CAREER-1 (800-227-3371); Fax: 201-848-1727. Email: mlewis@careerpress.com. Founded in 1985. Specialties: careers, job search (including Last Minute Tips), business (including The Smart Woman's Guides), education, personal finance, weddings, quotations, travel (50 Fabulous Places...), and reference.

27. Catbird Press, Robert Wechsler, Publisher, 16 Windsor Road, North Haven CT 06473, 203-230-2391. Email: catbird@pipeline.com. Since 1987, this literary press has specialized in Czech literature, sophisticated humor, and British and American fiction. While they don't always sell lots of copies of their books, they do well selling subsidiary rights.

28. Champion Press, Brook Noel, Editor, 4308 Blueberry Road, Fredonia WI 53021; 262-692-3897; Fax: 262-692-3342. Email: info@championpress.com. For submission guidelines, see their web site at: http://www.championpress.com/guidelines.htm. Do not email submissions. Publishes cookbooks, health books, and children's books. "We are looking for cookbooks and fitness titles that are especially geared toward a busy woman's lifestyle. We are also interested in new and innovating home management topics.

We publish a limited number of education and home schooling titles. We also publish self-help titles. We are no longer seeking submission in fiction, poetry or parenting.

Please send ONLY a proposal, including market analysis, marketing plan and ideas, your credential and bio, first 3 chapters and a SASE. Submissions without a SASE will not be returned. DO NOT PHONE OR E-MAIL. We get too many solicitations this way and thus do not reply.

Please follow our guidelines and be familiar with the types of books we publishing prior to sending your project our way. Address submissions to Attn: Editors. We have editorial meetings 4 times per year and your response will be sent within 60 days of the editorial meeting."

29. Charles River Media, David Pallai, President, 10 Downer Avenue, Hingham MA 02043; 781-740-0400; Fax: 781-740-8816. Email: info@charlesriver.com. Established in November 1994, Charles River Media publishes books and software supporting the Internet, networking, computer graphics, game development, programming, and computer engineering professional and educational markets.

30. Charlesbridge Publishing, Brent Farmer, Publisher, 85 Main Street, Watertown MA 02172; 617-926-0329; 800-225-3214; Fax: 617-926-5720. Talewinds is one of their imprints. Specialties: children's books: fiction, nature, environment, alphabet books. They also recently bought: Whispering Coyote Press, Alice "Lou" Alpert, 300 Crescent Court #1150, Dallas TX 75201; 214-871-5599; 800-929-6104; Fax: 214-871-5577.

31. Chelsea Green Publishing, John Barstow, Editor-in-Chief, 85 N Main Street #120, P O Box 428, White River Junction VT 05001; 802-295-6300; Fax: 802-295-6444. Email: jbarstow@chelseagreen.com. Web: http://www.chelseagreen.com. Ian and Margo Baldwin, founders. Specialties: nature, environment, gardening, independent living, alternative building technologies.

32. Chronicle Books — Jack Jensen, Publisher; Nion McEvoy, Editor-in-Chief; 85 Second Street, San Francisco CA

94105; 415-537-4460; 800-722-6657; Fax: 415-537-3730. Email: frontdesk@chronbooks.com. Specialties: "Chronicle Books specializes in high-quality, reasonably priced books for adults and children. Our titles include best-selling cookbooks; fine art, design, photography, and architecture titles; full-color nature books; award-winning poetry and literary fiction; regional and international travel guides; and gift and stationery items." They are a member of the Independent Book Publishers Hall of Fame.

33. Cimino Publishing Group, P O Box 174, Carle Place NY 11514; 516-997-3721; Fax: 516-997-3420. Email: cimpub@juno.com. Specialties: travel, music, cooking.

34. Clear Light Publishers, Harmon Houghton and Marcia Keegan, Publishers, 823 Don Diego, Santa Fe NM 87501; 505-989-9590; Fax: 505-989-9519. Email: clpublish@aol.com. Specialties: Native American, new age, Southwest cooking and culture.

35. Collectors Press, P O Box 230986, Portland OR 97281; 503-684-3030; 800-423-1848. Publish award-winning popular culture books and popular reference titles on art, science fiction, and other popular culture.

36. Common Courage Press, Liz Keith and Greg Bates, Publishers, 1 Red Barn Road, P O Box 702, Monroe ME 04951; 207-525-0900; Fax: 207-525-3068. Email: comcour@agate.net. Specialties: social justice issues.

37. Cool Springs Press, Roger Waynick, President, Franklin TN. Publishes regional cookbooks, gardening guides.

38. Copernicus Books, Paul Farrell, Editor-in-Chief, 37 East 7th Street, New York NY 10003; 212-228-0175, ext. 215; Fax: 212-995-0322. Email: pfarrell@copernicusbooks.com. Science and the application of science to interesting questions.

39. Craftsman Book Company, Gary Moselle, Publisher, 6058

Corte del Cedro, Carlsbad CA 92009; 760-438-7828; 800-829-8123; Fax: 760-438-0398.

40. Crane Hill Publishers, 3608 Clairmont Avenue, Birmingham AL 35222; 205-714-3007; Fax: 205-714-3008. Publishes regional titles.

41. Creative Publishing International, Alison Brown Cerier, Executive Editor, Lifestyles Group, 18705 Lake East Drive, Chanhassen MN 55317; 952-936-4700; 800-328-0590; Fax: 952-988-9101. Founded in 1969 as Cy DeCosse Incorporated, then bought by Cowles Enthusiast Media in 1994. In 1998, CPI was bought out by a management group and structured again as a private company. Their Singer Sewing Reference Library has sold 8,000,000 copies. They also publish other high-quality photographic books on crafts, home improvement, cooking, hunting, fishing, history, collectibles, equine, and healthy lifestyles. They also own NorthWord Press, another great publisher, and Two Can, a children's book company. Annual sales of $45 million. In summer 2004, they sold their how-to line (which includes books on home improvement, home decorating, and outdoors) to Rockport Publishers. They are a member of the Independent Book Publishers Hall of Fame.

42. Cross Cultural Publications, P O Box 506, Notre Dame IN 46556; 219-273-6526; 800-561-6526; Fax: 219-273-5973. Specialties: religion, social issues, international issues, cross cultural issues.

43. The Crossing Press, Elaine Goldman Gill, Publisher, 1201 Schaffer Road #B (Santa Cruz CA 95060), P O Box 1048, Freedom CA 95019; 831-420-1110; 800-777-1048; Fax: 831-420-1114. Email: crossing@crossingpress.com. Specialties: new age, holistic health, cookbooks, books for women, pet care, Native American, contemporary issues.

44. Cumberland House Publishing, One of their cookbooks

was a James Beard Cookbook of the Year.

45. Curiosity Kits, Scott Garrett, Publisher; Susan Magsamen, Editor (also founder and president); 11111 Pepper Road, P O Box 811, Hunt Valley MD 21031; 410-584-2605; 800-584-KITS; Fax: 410-584-1247. Email: ckitsinc@erols.com. They publish more than 60 craft book/kits exploring the arts, sciences, nature, make believe, and world cultures.

46. Davies-Black Publishing, Connie Kallback, Editor, 3803 E Bayshore Drive, Palo Alto CA 94303; 650-691-9123; 800-624-1765; Fax: 650-623-9271. Business books.

47. Down East Books, P O Box 679, Camden ME 04843-0679; 207-594-9544; 800-766-1670; Fax: 207-594-7215. Specialties: regional titles (art, photography, cooking, travel guides, children's books). Their Nimbus division specializes in nautical, sports, and nature titles. Their new Countrysport Press division specialzies in flyfishing, wingshooting, and gun dog titles.

48. Energize Inc., Susan Ellis, Publisher, 5450 Wissahickon Avenue, Philadelphia PA 19144-5221; 215-438-8342; 800-395-9800; Fax: 215-438-0434. Email: energize@energizeinc.com. Founded in 1977, they also publish the Volunteer Energy Resource Catalog. Specialties: volunteer management

49. M. Evans & Company, George de Kay, President, P.J. Dempsey, Senior Editor; 216 East 49th Street, New York NY 10017; 212-688-2810; Fax: 212-486-4544. Email: mevans@sprynet.com. Founded in 1963. Specialty: general trade books.

50. E-Z Legal Forms, Barry Chesler, President, 384 S Military Trail, Deerfield Beach FL 33442; 954-480-8933; Fax: 954-480-8906.

51. Fantagraphics Books, Gary Groth, President, 7563 Lake

City Way NE, Seattle WA 98115; 206-524-1967; 800-657-1100; Fax: 206-425-2104. Email: fbicomix@fantagraphics.com. Specialty: graphic novels and comics.

52. Firebrand Books, Karen Oosterhous, Publisher, 2232 S. Main Street #272, Ann Arbor MI 48103. Email: FirebrandBooks@comcast.net. Specialty: lesbian and feminist titles.

53. Focus Publishing, Ron Pullins, Publisher, 311 Merrimac Street, P O Box 369, Newburyport MA 01950; 978-462-7288; 800-848-7236; Fax: 978-462-9035. Email: pullins@pullins.com. Focus on college textbooks, the classics, philosophy, public policy, science, and drama.

54. Franklin, Beedle & Associates, Jim Leisy, Publisher, 8536 SW St Helens Drive #D, Wilsonville OR 97070; 503-682-7668; 800-322-2665; Fax: 503-682-7638. Having published 175 titles since 1985, they currently have 33 titles in print and average 10 new books per year. They specialize in publishing books on instruction, how-to, and reference for computers, including the Internet, operating systems, programming, and advanced computer systems.

55. Free Spirit Publishing, Judy Galbraith, President, 400 First Avenue N #616, Minneapolis MN 55401; 612-338-2068; 800-735-7323; Fax: 612-337-5050. Email: help4kids@freespirit.com. Founded in 1983. Specialties: resources for educators, parents, and children.

Ready to get those books stacked in your garage into the hands of even MORE readers? Earma has harnessed the power of Internet promotion into one place to set your book ablaze with new sales. Get the epackage Non-

Techie Ways to Market Your Book Online with software
bonuses that help you promote your book to a new
market - the WORLD. Visit here
http://bookmarketinghelp.com for details.

56. Fulcrum Publishing, Robert Baron, Publisher, 16100 Table Mountain Parkway #300, Golden CO 80403-1672; 303-277-1623; 800-992-2908; Fax: 303-279-7111. Email: fulcrum@fulcrum-books.com. Since 1984. Specialties: gardening, travel, nature, history, Native American studies, children's.

57. Gem Guides Book Company, 315 Cloverleaf Drive #F, Baldwin Park CA 91706; 626-855-1611; 800-824-5118; Fax: 626-855-1610. Email: gembooks@aol.com. Publishes and distributes books on rocks and minerals, jewelry making, Western interest, Native America, outdoor recreation, and travel.

58. Gibbs Smith, Publisher, Gibbs Smith, Publisher; Madge Baird, Editorial VP; 96 W Gentile Street, P O Box 667, Layton UT 84041; 801-544-9800; 800-748-5439; Fax: 801-544-5582. Email: info@gibbs-smith.com. Founded in 1969. Specialties: Western humor, cookbooks, Rocky Mountain regional titles, Native American, animals, architecture & design, nature, children's books, etc.

59. David R. Godine, Publisher, David Godine, Publisher. Founded in 1970, this publisher does about 30 titles per year. Specialties: general interest.

60. Golden West Publishers, Lee Fischer, 4113 N Longview, Phoenix AZ 85014; 602-265-4392; 800-658-5830; Fax: 602-279-6901. Specialties: regional, general.

61. Graphic Arts Center Publishing Company, Doug Pfeiffer, Associate Publisher, P O Box 10306, Portland OR 97296-0306; 503-226-2402; Fax: 503-223-1410. Tim Frew,

Executive Editor; Ellen Wheat, Senior Editor; Tricia Brown, Acquisitions Editor. Imprints: Alaska Northwest Books, Graphic Arts Center Publishing, WestWinds Press. They publish regional titles with national interest. Graphic Arts is known for its award-winning large format photography books, Alaska Northwest is Alaska's pioneer publisher and has been publishing everything Alaskan for over 40 years and, finally, WestWinds publishes titles on the West.

62. Gryphon House, Larry Rood, Publisher, P O Box 207, Beltsville MD 20704-0207; 301-595-9500; Fax: 301-595-0051. Specialties: early childhood books for teachers and parents.

63. Hampton Roads Publishing Company, Frank DeMarco, Chairman (Email: demarco@hrpub.com); Bob Friedman, Publisher, 1125 Stoney Ridge Road, Charlottesville VA 22902; 800-766-8009; Fax: 800-766-9042. Publishers of Neale Donald Walsch's Conversations with God, Book 2 Specialties: new age, visionary fiction.

64. Harvard Common Press, Bruce Shaw, Publisher, 535 Albany Street, Boston MA 02118; 617-423-5803; 888-657-3755; Fax: 617-695-9794. Specialty: cookbooks, parenting, childbirth.

65. Harvest House Publishers, 990 Owen Loop North, Eugene OR 97402-9173; 888-501-0160. Publishes Christian and gift books, including some bestsellers.

66. Hay House, Louise Hay, Publisher, P O Box 5100, Carlsbad CA 92018-5100; 800-654-5126. Specialty: New age books.

67. Health Information Press, Jim Davis, Publisher, Practice Management Information Corporation, 4727 Wilshire Boulevard #300, Los Angeles CA 90010; 323-954-0224; Fax: 323-954-0253. Founded in 1986. 200+ titles in print.

Specialties: health books for consumers, medical management books for doctors.

68. Hill Street Press, Tom Payton, Publisher, 191 E Broad Street #209, Athens GA 30601-2848; 706-613-7200; 800-295-0365; Fax: 706-613-7204. Email: payton@hillstreetpress.com. Founded in 1997, they publish a variety of regional titles. Their Hot Cross Books imprint publishes theme crossword puzzle books.

69. Hohm Press, Anthony Zuccarello, Publisher, P O Box, 2501, Prescott AZ 86302; 520-717-2944; 800-381-2700; Fax: 520-717-1779. Email: catalog@hohmpress.com. Founded in 1975. 63 titles in print. Specialty: holistic health, alternative lifestyles, spirituality, psychology, women's books, poetry, children's books.

70. Holloway House Publishing Group, 8060 Melrose Avenue, Los Angeles CA 90046; 323-653-8060; Fax: 323-655-9452. Email: psi@loop.com. Motto: World's largest publisher of black experience paperback books. Imprints: Holloway House, Melrose Square, Mankind, Avanti, and Premiere.

71. Human Kinetics, 1607 N Market Street, P O Box 5076, Champaign IL 61825-5076; 217-351-5076; 800-747-4457; Fax: 217-351-1549. Specialty: sports, coaching, physical activity.

72. Hunter House, Kiran Rana, Publisher, 1515 1/2 Park Street, P O Box 2914, Alameda CA 94501-0914; 510-865-5282; 800-266-5592; Fax; 510-865-4295. Email: info@hunterhouse.com. Specialties: health, family, community, social issues, psychology.

73. Illumination Arts, John Thompson, Publisher; Ruth Thompson, Editorial Director, 13256 Northup Way #9 (98005), P O Box 1865, Bellevue WA 98009; 425-644-7185. Email: liteinfo@illumin.com. A wonderful children's book publisher focusing on new age topics.

74. Impact Publishers, Robert Alberti, Editor and Publisher, P O Box 6016, Atascadero CA 93423-6016; 805-461-5917; 800-246-7228; Fax: 805-461-5919. Email: editor@impactpublishers.com. Specialty: psychology, self-help. They have published more than 100 titles and sold more than 3.3 million copies.

75. Inner Traditions, One Park Street, Rochester VT 05767; 802-767-3174; 800-246-8648; Fax: 802-767-3726. Specialties: new age, spiritual.

76. Intercultural Press, Toby Frank, President; David Hoopes, Editor; 374 U.S. Route 1, P O Box 700, Yarmouth ME 04096; 207-846-5168; 866-372-2665; Fax: 207-846-5181. Email: books@interculturalpress.com. Founded in 1980. Specialties: multicultural, intercultural relations. Practical guides and textbooks.

77. Island Press, P O Box 7, Covelo CA 95428; 707-983-6432; 800-828-1302; Fax: 707-983-6414. The environmental publisher.

78. Ivan R. Dee, Publisher, 1332 N Halsted Street, Chicago IL 60622-2694; 312-787-6262; Fax: 312-787-6269. Email: elephant@iranrdee.com. Established in 1988, this publisher of serious nonfiction books for general readers publishes about 50 titles per year. Imprints: Elephant Paperbacks and New Amsterdam Books. Series: Philosophers in 90 Minutes, Plays for Performance, and American Ways. Subject specialties: history, literature and letters, politics, biography, contemporary affairs, theatre and drama, philosophy. Also modern Russian literature, Holocaust studies, Judaic studies, religion, and African-American studies.

79. The Jewish Learning Group, 723 Montgomery Street, Brooklyn NY 11213; 888-56-LEARN. Jewish tradition and children's books only. Great covers.

80. Jewish Lights Publishing, Stuart Matlins, Publisher, Sunset Farm Offices, Route 4, P O Box 237, Woodstock VT 05091; 802-457-4000; 800-962-4544; Fax: 802-457-4004. Specialty: Jewish themes, spirituality, new age, healing, self-help.

81. JIST Works, J. Michael Farr, Publisher, 8902 Otis Avenue, Indianapolis IN 46216-1033; 317-613-4200; 800-648-5478; Fax: 317-264-3709. Email: jist-works@aol.com. Founded in 1981. Specialty: careers, job search. This company also distributes career books, tapes, and software to the school market.

82. Johnson Books, Barbara Johnson Mussil, Publisher; Stephen Topping, Editorial Director, 1880 South 57th Court, Boulder CO 80301; 303-443-9766; 800-258-5830; Fax: 303-443-1106. Email: books@jpcolorado.com. Specialties: regional, recreation, nature, archaeology, western history.

83. Judson Press, 800-331-1053; Fax: 610-768-2107. African-American books.

84. Just Us Books, Wade Hudson, President; Cheryl Hudson, Editor; 356 Glenwood Avenue, East Orange NJ 07017; 973-672-7701. Email: justusbook@aol.com. Specialties: children's books and learning materials from the Black experience.

85. Kidsbooks Inc., Vic Cavallaro, Publisher, 230 Fifth Avenue #1710, New York NY 10001; 800-890-7137; Fax: 800-890-7138. Founded in 1987, this company is now a $10 million per year business. Specialties: Children's books, pop-up books, lift-a-flap books, and SoftPlay interactive soft cloth books.

86. Krieger Publishing Company, Specialties: science, academic, education, politics.

87. Lerner Publishing, Adam Lerner, Publisher; Mary

Rodgers, Editor-in-Chief, 241 First Avenue N, Minneapolis MN 55401; 612-332-3344; 800-328-4929. Email: info@lernerbooks.com. This children's book publisher primarily publishes for the school and library markets. They have about 1,000 titles in print.

88. Llewellyn, Carl Weschcke, Publisher, P O Box 64383, St. Paul MN 55164-0383; 651-291-1970; 800-843-6666; Fax: 651-291-1908. Email: lwlpc@llewellyn.com. Specialty: new age and witchcraft books.

89. Longstreet Press, Scott Bard, Publisher; Suzanne De Galan and John Yow, Senior Editors; 2140 Newmarket Parkway #122, Marietta GA 30067; 770-980-1488; 800-927-1488; Fax: 770-859-9894. Recent bestseller: The Millionaire Next Door. Founded in 1988. 300 titles in print. Specialties: regional books, fiction, humor, contemporary life, gift books, gardening, travel, calendars, audiotapes, general.

90. MacAdam/Cage, David Poindexter, Publisher; Pat Walsh, Editor, 155 Sansome Street #620, San Francisco CA 94104; 415-986-7502; Fax: 415-986-7414. Bought MacMurray & Beck in October 2000. M&B has published National Book Award nominees. Specialties: quality fiction and narrative nonfiction (memoir, biography, etc.). Great covers! Divina, a second imprint, focuses on speculative and new age nonfiction, stories of soul.

91. Marlor Press, Marlin Bree, Publisher and Editorial Director; Loris Theovin Bree, President; 4304 Brigadoon Drive, St. Paul MN 55126; 612-484-4600; 800-669-4908; Fax: 612-490-1182. Email: marlor@minn.net. In business since 1982, this company has had at least one book on the Publishers Weekly Children's Bestsellers list. Specialty: marine, travel, nonfiction children's, gift journals.

92. McPherson & Company, Bruce McPherson, Editor and Publisher, P O Box 1126, Kingston NY 12402; 914-331-

5807; 800-613-8219. Email: bmcpher@ulster.net. McPherson & Company includes the imprints Documentext (art and culture titles), Treacle Press (the original name of the press), and Recovered Classics (reprints of lost works by 20th century authors). In addition to publishing contemporary American literary fiction and nonfiction, McPherson issues contemporary Italian fiction in English translation.

93. Meadowbrook Press, Bruce Lansky, Publisher, 5451 Smetana Drive, Minnetonka MN 55343; 612-930-1100; 800-338-2232; Fax: 612-930-1940. Specialty: parenting, childcare, and humor titles.

94. Mel Bay Publications, L. Dean Bye, 4 Industrial Drive, Pacific MO 63069; 314-257-3970; Fax: 314-257-5062. Specialty: music books, songbooks, and method books for all instruments. Also videos.

95. Menasha Ridge Press, Bob Sehlinger, Publisher, 700 South 28th Street #206, Birmingham AL 35233; 205-322-0439; Fax: 205-326-1012. Email: menasha@aol.com. Specialties: outdoors, travel, and dining books.

96. Meriwether Publishing, Ted Zapel, Editor, 885 Elkton Drive, Colorado Springs CO 80907; 719-594-4422; 800-937-5297; Fax: 719-594-9916. Email: merpcds@aol.com. Specialties: performing arts, theater, clowning.

97. The Millbrook Press, Howard Graham, 2 Old New Milford Road, Brookfield CT 06804; Fax: 516-287-5328. Specialty: children's books.

98. Morpheus International, James Cowan, President, 9250 Wilshire Boulevard, Beverly Hills CA 90212; 310-859-2557; Fax: 310-859-7455. Specialties: fantasy art books, calendars, posters, and gifts.

99. Mosaic Press, Howard Asher, Publisher, 85 River Rock Drive #202, Buffalo NY 14207; 800-387-8992; Fax: 800-

387-8992. Email: cp507@freenet.toronto.on.ca. A Canadian publisher of 450 titles with distribution in the United States. Specialties: international studies, social studies, art, architecture, music, theater, travel, and literature.

100. Mountain Press Publishing Company, John Rimel, Publisher, 1301 South 3rd Street W, P O Box 2399, Missoula MT 59806; 406-728-1900; 800-234-5308; Fax: 406-728-1635. Email: mtnpress@montana.com. Specialty: cowboys, geology, history, nature, regional, recreation.

101. Moyer Bell, Jennifer Moyer, Publisher, Kymbolde Way, Wakefield RI 02879; 401-789-0074; 888-789-1945; Fax: 401-789-3793. 125 titles in print. Specialties: fiction, literary essays.

102. Mustang Publishing, Rollin Riggs, Publisher, P O Box 770426, Memphis TN 38177; 901-684-1200; 800-250-8713; Fax: 901-684-1256. Email: info@mustangpublishing.com. Founded in 1983. Specialties: humor, parenting, sports, travel, general.

103. Mutual Publishing, Bennett Hymer, Publisher, 1215 Center Street #210, Honolulu HI 96816; 808-732-1709. Email: mutual@lava.net. The largest book publisher in Hawaii specializes in books about Hawaii.

104. Naiad Press, Barbara Grier, Publisher, P O Box 10543, Tallahassee FL 32302; 850-539-5965; Fax: 850-539-9731. Email: naiadpress@aol.com. Specialty: lesbian literature, fiction, and videos. The oldest and largest such publisher.

105. New Directions, Griselda Ohannessian, Publisher, 80 Eighth Avenue, New York NY 10011. Almost a non-profit publisher, this company was one of the first small independent publishers (founded in 1936). It is still a strong literary publisher with specialties in poetry as well as avant-garde fiction and nonfiction.

106. New Harbinger Publications, Patrick Fanning, President, 5674 Shattuck Avenue, Oakland CA 94609; 510-652-0215; 800-748-6273; Fax: 510-652-5472. Email: nhhelp@newharbinger.com. Founded in 1980.Specialties: books, audiotapes, and videos on psychology, health care, families, self-help.

107. New Horizon Press, Joan Dunphy, Publisher, P O Box 669, Far Hills NJ 07931; 908-604-6311; 800-533-7978; Fax: 908-604-6330. Specialties: true crime, self-help, children's self-help, current affairs, health, parenting, women's issues.

108. New World Library, Marc Allen, Publisher; Becky Benenate, Editorial Director; Georgia Hughes, Editor (email: georgia@nwlib.com); 14 Pamaron Way, Novato CA 94949; 415-884-2100; 800-972-6657; Fax: 415-884-2199. They have an active backlist of 150 titles. Specialty: new age books, holistic health, Native American, psychology, recovery, wellness, personal growth, quotations, and spoken-word audio.

109. Newmarket Press, Esther Margolis, Publisher, 18 East 48th Street #1501, New York NY 10017; 212-832-3575; 800-669-3903; Fax: 212-832-3629. Email: newmktprs@aol.com. Specialties: movie tie-ins, performing arts, parenting, personal finance, cooking, self-help, general.

110. No Starch Press, William Pollock, Publisher, 555 DeHaro Street #250, San Francisco CA 94107; 415-863-9900; Fax: 415-863-9950. Email: Bill@nostarch.com. Specialties: computer books. Great content and covers!

111. Northland Publishing, David Jenney, Publisher; Erin Murphy, Editor-in-Chief; 2900 N Fort Valley Road (86001), P O Box 1389, Flagstaff AZ 86002; 928-774-5251; 800-346-3257; Fax: 928-774-0592. Web: http://www.northlandpub.com. Rising Moon is their

specialty imprint for children's books. Specialties: regional, nature, children's books.

112. W W Norton & Company, 500 Fifth Avenue, New York NY 10110-0017; 212-354-5500; Fax: 212-869-0856; 800-223-4830. General titles with many college textbooks as well.

113. Nova Publishing, Dan Sitarz, Publisher, 1103 W College Street, Carbondale IL 62901; 618-457-3521; 800-748-1175; Fax: 618-457-2541. Email: dansitarz@earthlink.net. Founded 1987. Specialties: consumer law titles.

114. O'Reilly & Associates, Tim O'Reilly, Publisher, 1005 Gravenstein Highway N, Sebastopol CA 95472; 707-827-7000, 800-998-9938; Fax: 707-829-0104. Email: tim@oreilly.com. Starting out as a self-publisher of UNIX books, O'Reilly is now the fourth largest computer trade book publisher. Specialty: UNIX, software, computers. See also Travellers' Tales below. They are a member of the Independent Book Publishers Hall of Fame.

115. Open Horizons Publishing, John Kremer, Publisher, 1200 S. Main Street, P O Box 205, Fairfield IA 52556-0205; 641-472-6130; 800-796-6130; Fax: 641-472-1560. Email: info@bookmarket.com. Specialty: books on publishing and marketing. This publisher is here only because I made this list.

116. Orca Book Publishers, Andrew Wooldridge; U.S.: P O Box 468, Custer WA 98240; Canada: P O Box 5626, Victoria, British Columbia V8T 1C6 Canada; 800-210-5277; Fax: 250-380-1892. Email: orca@orcabook.com. Specialties: children's books and juvenile/teen fiction. They also distribute 8 other publishers. They only publish Canadian authors.

117. Overlook Press, Peter Mayer, Publisher, 386 W Broadway, 4th Floor, New York NY 10012; 212-965-8400;

Fax: 212-477-7525. Specialties: fiction, children's books, art, design, popular culture, etc.

118. The Overmountain Press, Their new Silver Dagger imprint publishes mysteries.

119. Paladin Press, Peder Lund, Publisher, Gunbarrel Tech Center, 7077 Winchester Circle, Boulder, CO 80301; 303-443-7250; Fax: 303-442-8741. Email: editorial@paladin-press.com. Founded in 1970. 600 titles in print. Specialty: military, guns, self-defense.

120. Palmer/Pletsch Publishing, Pati Palmer, President, P O Box 12046, Portland OR 97212-0046; 503-294-0696; 800-728-3784; Fax: 503-294-0695. 20 titles in print which have sold more than 2,000,000 books. Specialty: sewing books.

121. Para Publishing, Dan Poynter, Publisher, P O Box 8206, Santa Barbara CA 93118-8206; 805-968-7277; 800-PARAPUB; Fax: 805-968-1379; Fax-on-demand: 805-968-8957. Email: DanPoynter@ParaPublishing.com. Web: http://www.parapublishing.com. Founded in 1969. Specialties: publishing, writing, parachuting.

122. Parenting Press, Elizabeth Crary, Publisher, 11065 Fifth Avenue NE #F, P O Box 75267, Seattle WA 98125-4518; 206-364-2900; 800-992-6657; Fax: 206-364-0702. Email: fcrary@parentingpress.com. Founded in 1979. 55 titles in print. Specialty: parenting titles.

123. Peachtree Publishers, Margaret Quinlin, Publisher, 1700 Chattahooche Avenue, Atlanta GA 30318-2112; 404-876-8761. Specialties: children's, Southern regional (hiking, fishing, nature), and self-help, especially parenting. 60 to 70% of their 25 new titles each year are children's books, either picture books or young adult books.

124. Peel Productions, Doug DuBosque, Publisher, P O Box

546, Columbus NC 28722; 828-894-8838. Specializes in children's drawing books. They have sold over 6 million copies of the 60 titles they have published, with 51 of those titles still in print. They are not currently soliciting new submissions.

125. Pelican Publishing, Milburn Calhoun, Publisher; Nina Kooij, Editor, 1000 Burmaster Street, P O Box 3110, Gretna LA 70054; 504-368-1175; 800-843-1724 (order line only); Fax: 504-368-1195. Email: editorial@pelicanpub.com. Specialties: cookbooks, regional titles, editorial cartoons, children's, business, travel, general.

126. Penton Overseas, Hugh Penton, President, 2470 Impala Drive, Carlsbad CA 92008-7226; 760-431-0060; 800-748-5804; Fax: 760-431-8110. Email: info@pentonoverseas.com. Specialty: audiobooks on travel and language, especially overseas travel. But they also publish and distribute audiotapes on art, adventure, biography, business, and many other subjects.

127. The Permanent Press, Martin Shepard, Publisher, Noyac Road, Sag Harbor NY 11963; 516-725-1101; Fax: 516-725-1101. Also Second Chance Press. Specialty: quality fiction.

128. Picture Me Books, Deborah B. D'Andrea, P O Box 72054, Akron OH 44372; 330-762-6800; Fax: 330-762-2230. Email: Debbie@picture-me-books.com. Specialty: children's books. Currently have 43 titles in print. They sell not only to the bookstore market but also to photo, candy, toy, gift, mass, grocery, and drugstore markets. Also catalog, school fundraising, and premium sales. They sold over 850,000 books to Kodak and Walt Disney World for an anniversary promotion and 350,000 copies to Imation. Their Nibble Me Books were voted Product of the Year by the Professional Candy Buyers.

129. Pineapple Press, Specialties: Southeast regional titles, cookbooks.

130. PowerHouse Books, 180 Varick Street #1302, New York NY 10014; 212-604-9074; Fax: 212-366-5247. Specialties: Innovative photo, art, and pop culture illustrated books.

131. Pro-Action Sports, Stuart Sobel, Publisher, P O Box 26657, Los Angeles CA 90026; 213-666-7789; 888-567-7789; Fax: 213-666-3225. Email: dojo@proactionsports.com. Specialty: martial arts books and videos.

132. Prometheus Books, Steven Mitchell, Editor in Chief, 59 John Glenn Drive, Amherst NY 14228-2197; 800-421-0351; Fax: 716-691-0137. Email: editorial@prometheusbooks.com. Specialties: real science, debunking of pseudoscience, human rights, social issues, psychology, exposés. They recently bought the backlist titles of Humanities Press and have launched a new imprint, Humanity Books, to publish books on philosophy and social science. Prometheus publishes about 100 new titles per year. Lou Anders is the editor of their Pyr Science Fiction and Fantasy line of novels.

133. Pruett Publishing Company, Jim Pruett, Publisher, 2928 Pearl Street, Boulder CO 80301; 303-449-4919; Fax: 303-433-9019. Email: pruettbks@aol.com. Specialties: regional, nature, travel, outdoor recreation, history.

134. Publications International, J. Robert Stank, Publisher, 7373 N Cicero Avenue, Lincolnwood IL 60646; 847-676-3470; Fax: 847-676-3671. Specialties: cookbooks, consumers, children's books, sports, entertainment, crafts, lifestyles, health and fitness, general. They are a member of the Independent Book Publishers Hall of Fame.

135. Pushcart Press, Bill Henderson, Publisher, P O Box 380, Wainscott NY 11975-0380; 516-324-9300. Specialties:

stories, fiction, publishing, general.

136. QED Press, 155 Cypress Street, Fort Bragg CA 95437; 707-964-9520; Fax: 707-964-7531. Email: qedpress@cypresshouse.com. 41 titles. Founded 1984. Mission statement: QED Press is a small, award-winning West Coast publishing house whose vision is to publish non-fiction and fiction that inpires readers to transcend national, racial and ethnic boundaries through an appreciation of the humanities, world literature, art, and poetry.

137. Quail Ridge Press, Gwen McKee, Editor, P O Box 123, Brandon MS 39043; 800-343-1583; Fax: 800-864-1082. Email: info@quailridge.com. Publishes cookbooks, the Mississippi mystery series, some children's books.

138. Quality Medical Publishing, 2248 Welsch Industrial Court, Saint Louis MO 63146; 314-878-7808. Email: customerservice@qmp.com. Publisher of award-winning medical books, journals and digital media in plastic surgery, spine surgery, otolaryngology, neurosurgery, dermatology, and orthopedic surgery.

139. Quill Driver Books, Steve Blake Mettee, Publisher, 1254 Commerce Avenue, Sanger CA 93657; 559-876-2170; Fax: 559-876-2180. Email: info@quilldriverbooks.coms. Also Word Dancer Press. Specialties: regional, history, writing, books for people over 50.

140. RDR Books, Roger Rapoport, Publisher, 4456 Piedmont Avenue, Oakland CA 94611; 510-595-0595; Fax: 510-595-0598. Email: rdrbooks@lanminds.com. They have two imprints: Wetlands Press publishes literary and innovative children's books; Zenobia Press publishes books by women or about women's issues. They also publish the humorous Wannabe Guides and travel humor/travel guides.

141. Red Wheel/Weiser, Michael Kerber, President, 368 Congress Street, 4th Floor, Boston MA 02210; 617-542-1324; 800-423-7087; Fax: 617-482-9676. New age, philosophy, spirituality, etc.

142. Redleaf Press, Eileen Nelson, 450 N Syndicate #5, St. Paul MN 55104; 612-641-6629; Fax: 612-645-0990. 310 titles. Specialties: early childhood, child care.

143. Roberts Rinehart, Jack Van Zandt, Publisher; Betsy Armstrong, Editor-in-Chief; 6309 Monarch Park Place #101, Niwot CO 80503; 303-652-2685; 800-352-1985; Fax: 303-652-2689. Specialties: general, nature, ecology, Ireland (especially through their division, Irish American Book Company, Email: IrishBooks@aol.com), fiction, travel, art and photography, children's books.

144. Sandlapper Publishing, Amanda Gallman, Publisher, 1281 Amelia Street, Orangeburg SC 29115; 803-531-1658; Fax: 803-534-5223. Email: agallman1@mindspring.com. Established in 1983, this regional publisher issues up to 6 new titles each year, with 100 titles in backlist. This company also distributes more than 300 titles from other publishers. They are mostly interested in titles about South Carolina or the South. No fiction, poetry, or politics.

145. Santa Monica Press, Jeffrey Goldman, Publisher, P O Box 1076, Santa Monica CA 90406-1076; 310-230-7759; 800-784-9553; Fax: 310-230-7761. Email: smpress@pacificnet.net. General how-to and offbeat books. Still doing a wonderful job marketing off-beat books to catalogs and non-book retailers.

146. Sasquatch Books, Chad Haight, Publisher, 615 Second Avenue #260, Seattle WA 98104; 800-775-0817; Fax: 206-467-4301. Founded in 1986. Publishes 40 new titles per year. Specialties: cookbooks, gardening, regional titles, general.

147. Scaledown, Brenda Ponichtera, 1519 Hermits Way, The Dales OR 97058; 541-296-5859; Fax: 541-296-1875. Email: scaledwn@gorge.net. This company doesn't qualify by number of titles published, but self-publisher Brenda has done such a wonderful job of promoting her cookbooks that I've decided she deserves a spot on this list. Check out her Quick & Healthy cookbooks which have sold more than half a million copies!

148. Self-Counsel Press, Richard Day, Managing Editor, 1704 N State Street, Bellingham WA 98225; 360-676-4530; 877-877-6490; Fax: 360-676-4549. Email: admin@self-counsel.com. This Canadian publisher publishes books on self-help law for the layperson, business, marketing, family/lifestyle, and writing.

149. Seven Locks Press, Jim Riordan, Publisher, 3100 W Warner Avenue #8, P O Box 25689, Santa Ana CA 92799; 714-545-2526; 800-354-5348; Fax: 714-545-1572. Email: sevenlocks@aol.com. Specialties: contemporary issues, coffee table books, gift books, celebrities, Native American.

150. Shambhala Publications, 300 Massachusetts Avenue, Boston MA 02115; 617-424-0030; 888-424-2329; Fax: 617-236-1563. Email: editors@shambhala.com. Specialty: Buddhism, new age titles, Eastern philosophy, holistic health, psychology, yoga, martial arts. Publishes 60 to 85 titles per year.

151. Silverback Books, Howard Cohl, President, 11601 Wilshire Boulevard #1500, Los Angeles CA 90025; 310-479-1555; Fax: 310-479-1561. Email: hcohl@silverbackbooks.com.

152. Snow Lion Publications, Jeff Cox, President, 605 West State Street, P O Box 6483, Ithaca NY 14851, 607-273-8519. Email: Tibet@SnowLionPub.com. Snow Lion publishes books on Tibet and Tibetan Buddhism.

153. Sourcebooks Inc., Dominique Raccah, Publisher, 1935 Brookdale Road #139, Naperville IL 60563; 630-961-3900 #224; 800-727-8866; Fax: 630-961-2168. Email: dominique.raccah@sourcebooks.com. Founded in 1987. Imprints: Casablanca Press, Hysteria, Sphinx Publishing. Specialties: general, children's, romance, beauty, fiction, multimedia. The fastest growing independent publisher out there.

154. Spinsters Ink, Sharon Silvas, Editorial Director, P O Box 2200, Denver CO 80222; 303-761-5552; 800-301-6860. Email: fempres@aol.com. Specialty: lesbian and feminist fiction.

155. Square One Books, Rudy Shur, Publisher, 115 Herricks Road, Garden City Park NY 11040; 516-535-2010; Fax: 516-535-2014. Email: sq1info@aol.com. Books on writing, health, cooking, and more.

156. Stackpole Books, 5067 Ritter Road, Mechanicsburg PA 17055; 717-796-0411; 800-732-3669; Fax: 717-796-0412. Email: sales@stackpolebooks.com. Specialties: nature, outdoor recreation and sports, history, military reference, and Pennsylvania.

157. Starburst Publishers, David and Sharon Robie, Publishers, P O Box 4123, Lancaster PA 17604; 717-293-0939; Fax: 717-293-1945. Email: starburst@starburstpublishers.com. Specialties: inspiration, self-help, health, religious.

158. Steerforth Press, Chip Fleischer, 25 Lebanon Street, Hanover NH 03755; 603-643-4787; Fax: 607-643-4788. Email: info@steerforth.com. Specialties: general fiction and nonfiction.

159. Stemmer House Publishers, Barbara Holdridge, 2627 Caves Road, Owings Mills MD 21117; 410-363-3690; Fax: 410-363-8459. Specialty: children's books, design.

160. Gareth Stevens Inc., Gareth Stevens, Publisher, 330 W Olive Street, Milwaukee WI 53212; 414-332-3520; Fax: 414-332-3567. Email: info@gsinc.com. Founded in 1983. 600 titles in print. Specialty: children's books.

161. Stillpoint Publishing, Meredith Young-Sowers, Publisher, Meetinghouse Road, P O Box 640, Walpole NH 03608; 603-756-9281; 800-847-4014; Fax: 603-756-9282. Email: stillpoint@top.monad.net. Founded in 1983. 50 titles in print.

162. Stoeger Publishing, 17603 Indian Head Highway #200, Accokeek MD 20607; 301-283-6981; Fax: 310-283-4783. "Stoeger Publishing is the nation's foremost publisher of outdoor, hunting, fishing and firearms books. Located in historic southern Maryland, Stoeger Publishing is dedicated to the production of quality books at a great price for outdoor sports enthusiasts worldwide. Since 1924, Stoeger has published or distributed hundreds of titles, most notably the signature annuals Shooter's Bible and Gun Trader's Guide." It's books have won many awards as well as hit several bestseller lists, including the New York Times, Nielsen BookScan, and Mid-South Booksellers Association.

163. Stone Bridge Press, Peter Goodman, Publisher, P O Box 8208, Berkeley CA 94707; 510-524-8732; Fax: 510-524-8711. Email: sbp@stonebridge.com. Specialties: Japanese themes.

164. Sunstone Press, James Clois Smith, Jr., Publisher, P O Box 2321, Santa Fe NM 87504-2321; 800-243-5644; Fax: 505-988-1025. Email: jsmith@sunstonepress.com. Publishes novels, Native American, health, cookbooks, regional, and children's books.

165. Sybex, Jordan Gold, VP Publishing, 1151 Marina Village Parkway, Alameda CA 94501; 510-523-8233, Fax: 510-523-1766. Email: info@sybex.com. Also web:

http://www.sybexgames.com. Rodnay Zaks, Founder. Founded in 1976, Sybex publishes books on computers (certification, database management, graphic eesign/multimedia, game strategy guides, Internet/www, operating systems, office software, programming). Its books are available in more than 25 languages.

166. Ten Speed Press, Phil Woods, President; Lorena Jones, Editorial Director, 999 Harrison Street, P O Box 7123, Berkeley CA 94707; 510-559-1600; 800-841-BOOK; Fax: 510-559-1629. Specialties: health, cooking, careers, new age. Imprints: Celestial Arts, Crossing Press, and Tricycle Press.

167. Third World Press, Haki Madhubuti, Publisher, 7822 S Dobson Avenue, Chicago IL 60619; 773-651-0700; Fax: 773-651-7286. Specialty: African American themes.

168. Tilbury House Publishers, Jennifer Elliott, Publisher, 2 Mechanic Street #3, Gardiner ME 04345; 207-582-1899; 800-582-1899; Fax: 207-582-8227. Email: tilbury@tilburyhouse.com. Specialties: general.

169. J. N. Townsend Publishing, Jeremy Townsend, Publisher, 12 Greenleaf Drive, Exeter NH 03833; 603-778-9883; 800-333-9883. Email: JNTown@aol.com. Specialty: animal and nature books.

170. Travelers' Tales, James O'Reilly, Editor and Associate Publisher, 853 Alma Street, Palo Alto CA 94301; 650-462-2110; Fax: 650-462-2114. Email: ttales@travelerstales.com. Founded in 1993, this company is owned by the same family who owns O'Reilly & Associates (see above). They have won the Lowell Thomas Award for best travel book three times in their five-year history. Specialties: travel (especially travel stories), travel humor, misadventure, romance, and food.

171. Vacation Spot Press, Cheryl Barnes, Publisher, P O Box

17011, Alexandria VA 22302; 703-684-8142; Fax: 703-684-7955. Email: mail@vspbooks.com. Publishes children's poetry books, including several New York Times bestsellers by 11-year-old Mattie Stepanek, a victim of muscular distrophy.

172. Visible Ink Press, 835 Penobscot Building, 645 Griswold Street, Detroit MI 48226-4094; 800-776-6265. Reference titles: movies, TV, entertainment, nature, and more.

173. Volcano Press, Adam Gottstein, Publisher, 21376 Consolation Street, P O Box 270, Volcano CA 95689; 209-296-3445; 800-879-9636; Fax: 209-296-4515. Ruth Gottstein, Editorial Consultant. Email: ruth@volcanopress.com. Specialties: women's health, family violence issues, and multicultural children's books.

174. Westcliffe Publishers, P O Box 1261, Englewood CO 80150-1261; 303-935-0900; Fax: 303-935-0903. Email: sales@westcliffepublishers.com. Specialty: High quality natural landscape publications.

175. Wilderness Press, 1200 5th Street, Berkeley CA 94710-1306; 510-558-1666; Fax: 510-558-1696. Outdoor books and maps.

176. Workman Publishing Company, Peter Workman, Publisher, 708 Broadway, New York NY 10003; 212-254-5900; 800-722-7202; Fax: 212-254-8098. Also owns Algonquin Books of Chapel Hill. This is the premier pioneering publisher of trade paperbacks and Page-a-Day calendars. A standard setter who has sold millions of copies of dozens of titles. They are a member of the Independent Book Publishers Hall of Fame.

177. World Leisure, Charles Leocha, Publisher, 177 Paris Street, Boston MA 02128 (P.O. Box 160, Hampstead NH 03841); 617-569-1966; 800-292-1966; Fax: 617-561-7654. Email: wleisure@aol.com. Specialty: travel books.

178. Zagat Survey, Eugene (Tim) Zagat, Publisher, 4 Columbus Circle, New York NY 10019-1107; 800-333-3421; Fax: 212-977-6488. Email: zagat@zagatsurvey.com. Specialty: restaurant and hotel guide books.

Appendix IV

POD PUBLISHING SERVICE COMPARISON DIRECTORY

*Non-Exclusive Contract
**Online Sales – Amazon, BN.com, Books-A-Million, etc

Don't forget to visit the Resource section at the end of this book for a blank POD Publisher's checklist to make your own comparisons. Now compare the top 4 companies (at the time of this writing – be sure to check current pricing) and choose wisely:

Excerpt Marketing from Top POD Publishing Websites:

1. iUniverse Publishing
The Select Publishing Package $599 $99   extra   for eBook format: http://www.iuniverse.com

Included w/ this pkg

The Select publishing package is an economical choice for authors just entering the self-publishing arena. With the Select package, you'll receive a custom cover—including artwork or photographs—at no extra charge. Your book will be available for order from the iUniverse online bookstore, Barnes and Noble.com, and from over 25,000 bookstores and e-retailers worldwide. Plus, you can customize your publishing experience by adding a wide variety of optional services both during the production process and after your book is completed.

The Select Package Includes:

- Marketing toolkit
- Custom designed cover

- Paperback formatting
- eBook formatting
- Volume discounts for author book purchases
- Five (5) free paperback copies of your book
- ISBN assignment
- Worldwide distribution
- Inclusion in the iUniverse online bookstore
- One-on-one author support
- Non-exclusive contract

2. Author House

Standard Option $599

http://www.authorhouse.com

Included w/ Standard Option

Join the growing community of over 20,000 authors who have made AuthorHouse their source for premier self-publishing services. Let AuthorHouse guide you through the publishing process and tailor your manuscript to meet your vision. Standard Paperback Publishing is ideal for chronicling your life in an autobiography, capturing savory recipes in a cookbook, composing a book of poetry, writing your first novel...or your fiftieth!

Program Details

- **Full-color cover design**. Match the beauty of the written word with a cover proposed by you and created by AuthorHouse.
- **Black and white interior format**. Whether in scholarly libraries or on relaxing beaches, readers will have your book in the format they have come to love...the classic paperback. Or, upgrade to hard cover and give your book

the distinguished look it deserves.

- **Full interior text layout**. Control the look of every page with a text layout of your choice.
- **ISBN distribution number**.

Technical Details

Formats available: 5" x 8", 6" x 9" and 8.25" x 11"

Page counts: For the 5" x 8" and 6" x 9" formats the allowable page count is from 48 to 740 pages. For the 8.25" x 11" format the allowable page count is from 48 to 828 pages.

Hard cover upgrade: If upgrading to the 6" x 9" hard cover with dust jacket, the allowable page count is from 108 to 740 pages.

3. Xlibris
Basic Service $649
www.xlibris.com

Included in basic service:

Overview

The Basic Service allows you some control of your book's look by giving you choices of cover and interior templates. Choose from 8 Cover Templates and 5 Interior Templates to customize your book. This service comes in paperback formats. The price of the Basic Service is $500.

- Your choice of 8 Cover Templates
- Your choice of 5 Interior Templates
- Ability to supply an image for the cover of your book
- Ability to submit an Author Photo for your cover
- A trade paperback Author Review copy
- Availability in e-book format (Adobe Acrobat Reader)

Also Included:

- Book Formats: trade paperback
- ISBN Numbers and UPC barcode
- Registration with: Amazon.com, Borders.com, BarnesandNoble.com, Ingram, Books in Print, and more than 200 online stores
- Electronic galleys
- Paperback royalties: 25% of cover price (direct sales), 10% (Distributor/Reseller sales)
- Author discounts of 40% on trade paperbacks
- A public Author Web Page
- A public Book Web Page
- Control over your book excerpt viewable in Xlibris' Online bookstore
- Online Book Sales Reporting
- Custom book URL registration
- You can purchase Add-Ons to add corrections, images, and more

4. Infinity Publishing Company

Basic pkg $499

http://www.infinitypublishing.com

Included in basic pkg:

In the publishing of your book, we charge a one-time setup fee of only $499. For this, your book will be entered into our printing and publishing system, registered in "books in print", get a custom-made barcode, be assigned an ISBN, get a top quality cover design, and be shipped to you as a real, hardcopy book in about 8 weeks from submission. It will be made available for sale on our ecommerce Web site, submitted to amazon.com and others, and sold to bookstores on a returnable basis (which is usually one of their requirements). We will then pay you royalties each month on all sales of your book. There are no hidden charges.

Extended Distribution - $149: Our basic publishing service will make your book available to consumers in a wide variety of places. However, ordering this additional package will see it submitted to Ingram for inclusion in their LSI (Lighting Source Incorporated) printing and distributions systems. This means that your book will be available to consumers at even more stores and retail web sites.

Other Companies

20 companies (alphabetized) with active links to consider are:

1. AuthorHouse
2. Aventine Press
3. Black Forest Press
4. Booklocker.com, Inc
5. BookPublisher.com
6. ButterflyPress.net
7. Cold Tree Press
8. First Books
9. Infinity Publishing
10. iUniverse
11. Llumina Press
12. LuLu
13. PageFree Publishing, Inc.
14. Publish America
15. Tabby House
16. Universal Publishers
17. Unlimited Publishing
18. WinePress Publishing
19. Xlibris

20. Xulon Press

I hope this information is helpful to you. It helped me make an informed choice when I knew nothing about the industry of publishing. Here's to the success of your book publishing dreams!

Appendix V

SELF PUBLISHING GLOSSARY

Plain English glossary of *Self-Publishing Terms.*

Note: All time frames, percentages and amounts are provided for example purposes only. They are not given as an indication of what you should expect in a POD publishing contract. Please seek your own legal and accounting advice before engaging in any business activity or entering any legal contract.

1. **AFFILIATES** means owners, shareholders, officers, directors, employees, parents, subsidiaries, affiliated companies, licenses, distributors, advertisers, Internet service providers, attorneys, and accountants and any other person or entity to whom PUBLISHER extends its license or warranties to in connection with the production, dissemination, transmission, promotion, publication, or distribution of the WORK or the exercise of any rights therein or derived there from.

2. **AUTHOR CANCELLATION.** This sections explains the AUTHOR'S right to cancel. *Example:* AUTHOR has the right at any time to cancel this agreement with thirty (30) days advance written notice to the PUBLISHER. If the AUTHOR chooses to cancel, the PUBLISHER will have the nonexclusive right to exercise the licensed rights granted in (LICENSE OF RIGHTS) above one (1) year following the receipt of the cancellation notice.

3. **AUTHOR WARRANTIES.** Author Warranties are where the author guarantees to the PUBLISHER things like they are the sole owner with full legal rights to enter into an

agreement. Additionally, the AUTHOR guarantees the work is free of conflict, obscenity, legal restrictions and do not violate anyone's copyright.

Example: AUTHOR represents and warrants the following to the PUBLISHER: (i) AUTHOR is the sole owner of the WORK (including any associated cover or interior graphics supplied by the AUTHOR) and has the full power, authority and right to enter into this Agreement; (ii) this Agreement does not conflict with any arrangements, understandings, or agreements between the AUTHOR and any other person or entity; (iii) the WORK is not in the public domain and is entirely original except for portions thereof for which legally the effective written licenses or permissions have been secured...

4. **BACK MATTER.** The text that occurs after the last chapter in the book (or the main body of text). Back matter often comprises such parts as the index, endnotes, author biography, bibliography, etc. The pages are numbered with Arabic numerals.

5. **BLEED.** If you have an image that you want to print to the edge of the book, then that image "bleeds". This is often done on book covers. For the printer to be able to trim the books so that the image is at the edge there must be some part of the image that gets trimmed off (or else you will have a white stripe of the paper showing).

   The amount that gets trimmed off is the "bleed", and printers require a minimum of 1/8" (¼" is preferable). So, be sure that you set up your files so that you have enough image to go beyond your trim. In other words, a 6 x 9" cover that bleeds all 3 sides on the front will really be a minimum of 6-1/8 x 9-1/4".

6. **CAMERA READY COPY:** A printed copy of your manuscript that is ready to go to press, in the proper format that is required for your printer.

7. **CIP.** Cataloging in Publication information is the bibliographic information supplied by the Library of Congress and printed on the copyright page. Librarians use this information when adding new titles to their collections.

8. **COMB-BINDING.** A plastic "spiral" is inserted into holes drilled directly into edge of book pages. Book will open flat for easy reading.

9. **COOPERATIVE PUBLISHER.** Recently, a hybrid of a book packager and a subsidy publisher, called a cooperative publisher, has emerged in the marketplace. Like the book packager, the author enters into a publishing agreement with the cooperative publisher to produce a fixed number of books for a fixed amount of dollars. When the printing is complete, a certain number of these books are the sole property of the author and the rest are used for joint marketing and sales.

   This agreement is for a fixed period of time during which, if the book sells out, the cooperative publisher will reprint the book at his expense. Royalties of 50% of net revenue on the initial printing are paid twice a year. As with the subsidy press, the author uses the cooperative publisher's ISBN number.

10. **FRONT MATTER.** The text that occurs before the first chapter in the book (or the main body of text). Front matter often comprises such parts as the dedication, acknowledgments, table of contents, etc. The pages are numbered with Roman numerals.

11. **GENERAL PROVISIONS.** General Provisions usually cover anything the contract writer may have missed, misrepresented or not written correctly.

   Example: If any term or provision of this Agreement is illegal or unenforceable, then, nonetheless, this Agreement shall remain in full force and effect and such term or provision shall be deemed deleted or curtailed only to such extent as is necessary to make it legal or enforceable. This agreement represents the complete understanding between the parties as to its subject matter and supersedes all prior understanding, if nay, as to its subject matter. No modification, amendment, or waiver shall be valid or binding unless made in writing and signed by all parties hereto.

12. **GOVERNING LAW.** The AUTHOR agrees to the PUBLISHER'S governing law.

    Example: This Agreement shall be governed by the internal laws of the State of California as a contract fully executed and to be performed in Santa Clara County, California, without regard to conflict of laws rules, and shall bind and benefit the applicable heirs, successors, assigns, and personal representatives of the parties hereto, though AUTHOR may not assign this Agreement or any rights or obligations hereunder, by operation of law or any other manner, with the PUBLISHER'S prior written consent, such consent not to be unreasonably withheld.

13. **HARD-BOUND.** Hard cover book binding, usually vinyl covering over cardboard.

14. **IMPRINT.** The company name under which your book is being published (e.g., Greenleaf Book Group Press, Penguin Classics, etc.).

15. **INDEMNIFICATION OF THE PUBLISHER.** This statement is where the AUTHOR agrees to hold harmless the PUBLISHER and its affiliates from any losses, damages, liabilities, etc. **Example:** Indemnification of the publisher is where the AUTHOR agrees fully indemnify, defend and hold harmless the PUBLISHER and its AFFILIATES from and against any losses, lost profits, damages, liabilities, judgments, awards, decrees, settlements, or

expenses (including without limitation, reasonable attorney's fees and court costs) arising from, connected with, or by reason of any breach or alleged breach of any of the representations and warranties set forth above, but the AUTHOR shall not be liable for any matter inserted in the WORK by the PUBLISHER or its licensees. All warranties and indemnification made by the AUTHOR herein shall survice termination of this Agreement or any license hereunder.

16. **ISBN.** The International Standard Book Number is a unique thirteen-digit number assigned to every book and obtained from the R. R. Bowker company. This is the number most often used to order a book or keep track of it in the supply chain.

17. **LICENSE OF RIGHTS.** License of Rights is also the license to publish.

    Example: AUTHOR gives the PUBLISHER the non-exclusive, worldwide license to publish the WORK in print, in whole or in part, in the English language. The AUTHOR also gives the the PUBLISHER the right to make the work viewable on the PUBLISHER's web site, or partner web sites that have entered into agreement with the PUBLISHER, in order to facilitate sales of the WORK

18. **LCCN.** The Library of Congress Control Number is the Library of Congress's system of uniquely numbering books. Librarians use this information to access the book's correct cataloging data.

19. **NON-EXCLUSIVE RIGHTS.** Non-Exclusive Rights means the AUTHOR keeps ownership of their work. **Example:** AUTHOR gives the PUBLISHER the non-exclusive, worldwide license to publish the WORK in print, in whole or in part, in the English language.

20. **NOTICES.** This sections states how all notices should be handled.

    Example: All notices must be given in writing and sent by fax or overnight courier (e.g., FedEx, UPS, or DHL) to AUTHOR's address and fax number specified below and to PUBLISHER's addresses and fax number displayed at PUBLISHER'S web site on the date of notice.

21. **PARTIES TO THE CONTRACT.** This AUTHOR and PUBLISHER entering into a contractual agreement.

    Example: This is a Publishing Agreement between the author (AUTHOR) listed below and Some Publishing Company, Inc. with its principal offices at 2000 Any Street, A City, 78612 (PUBLISHER) for the WORK listed at the end of this Agreement (WORK)

22. **PERFECT BINDING.** A process of binding pages into a book cover. Used in production of paperback novels.

23. **PRINT ON DEMAND BOOK PRINTING.** On-demand publishers set up your digital manuscript to be printed one book at a time using a Docu-tech. You pay a set fee of between $350 and $1,250 and receive in return one hardback copy of your book and one softback copy. If they set the retail price of the softback at $18, say, then each additional book you order from them costs you $10.80 (40% off the retail price). If a bookstore, wholesaler, or on-line bookseller orders your book, you receive a royalty ranging from $1 to $2.30 per book.

24. **PUBLICATION.** This section explains the publisher's terms for publishing a work.

    Example: The PUBLISHER intends to make the WORK available for print-distribution within ninety (90) days after receipt of all required materials relating to the WORK, but in no case later than one hundred eighty (180) days after the receipt of all the required materials relating to the WORK. If the PUBLISHER does not make the WORK available with such time, except for delays caused by external circumstances beyond its control, the AUTHOR may give written notice to the PUBLISHER to make the WORK available within thirty (30) days. If the PUBLISHER does not do, this AGREEMENT shall terminate and all rights herein granted shall revert to the AUTHOR.

25. **PUBLICATION FORMAT.** The publisher states how they will handle formatting or typesetting your book. **Example:** PUBLISHER shall have full discretion as to price, production, appearance and formats of the WORK.

26. **RENEW AUTOMATIC.** Renew Automatic is where the PUBLISHER gives you their intent to renew the license to publish automatically after a certain length of time unless advance written notice is given.

    Example: The license will automatically renew for consecutive _____ year terms if neither party gives at least thirty (30) days advance written notice, prior to the end of the current term that it desires to terminate.

27. **ROYALTIES.** This term explains what the author is paid.

    Example: On all sales of printed copies of the WORK, the PUBLISHER will pay the AUTHOR a royalty equal to 20% of the payments the PUBLISHER actually receives from sales of printed copies of the WORK, less any shipping and handling charges, sales and use taxes, and returns. Royalties will not be paid on copies provided or sold to the AUTHOR.

28. **ROYALTY PAYMENTS.** Royalty payments explain when and how often the author is paid.

    Example: PUBLISHER will make four annual royalty payments, if earned, to the AUTHOR within sixty (60) days of the end of each calendar quarter. If the royalty payment due in a single calendar quarter is less than twenty-five US Dollars ($25), at which time the PUBLISHER shall make the appropriate royalty payment to the AUTHOR.

29. **RETAIN.** All publication rights not explicitly granted to the PUBLISHER are reserved to the AUTHOR.

30. **SADDLE STICHING.** Usually used on smaller page quantities, book pages are "stitched" or stapled in two or three places on fold.

31. **SUBSIDY PRESS.** Also known as a vanity press, is a publishing company that applies its ISBN to a book and charges the author for the cost of production. The author receives only a few copies of the book, and is promised royalties on those copies that might be sold by the subsidy press.

32. **TERM.** The Term explains the length of license to publish.

    Example: The license for the WORK shall extend for three (3) years after the date the PUBLISHER first releases it for publication. The license will automatically renew for consecutive one (1) year terms if neither party gives at least thirty (30) days advance written notice, prior to the end of the current term that it desires to terminate.

33. **TRIM..** This is the physical dimension (measured in width and length) of your book after the printer has cut it to the desired size. Common trim sizes include 8.5 x 11, 5.5 x 8.5, and 6 x 9—in the United States, they're always measured in inches.

34. **TERM OF COPYRIGHT.** Term of Copyright is where the PUBLISHER agrees to post for the WORK the copyright name given by AUTHOR and secure a unique ISBN.

    Example: PUBLISHER agrees to post for the WORK the

copyright name specified by AUTHOR and secure a unique ISBN.

35. **USE OF AUTHOR'S NAME AND LIKENESS.** The AUTHOR agrees to allow PUBLISHER to use his name and likeness in promotional items or events.

Example: The PUBLISHER may post pertinent information regarding AUTHOR or WORK. The information may include elements of the title submission package, such as author biographical sketch and description of the WORK. The PUBLISHER may also post additional information that will help promote the AUTHOR or WORK. If the PUBLISHER requests such information, the AUTHOR agrees to promptly provide the information.

36. **PUBLISHER BANKRUPTCY.** This statement explains what happens to the AUTHOR'S rights if the PUBLISHER goes bankrupt.

Example: If the PUBLISHER commences bankruptcy proceedings, all rights to the WORK shall immediately revert to the AUTHOR.

37. **VANITY PUBLISHER**. A publisher that publishes a book at the expense of the author.

38. **VELO-BINDING.** A plastic strip along front cover. Book will NOT open flat.

Appendix VI

PUBLISH ON DEMAND CHECKLIST

Here are some things to consider when choosing your POD publisher. Not all companies offer the same options. You decide which options mean the most to you in making your decision:

__Y/N__   __OPTIONS__

1.   _____Contract (Non-exclusive)

2.   _____Interior Text Format Included?

3.   _____eBook Included or Available?

4.   _____ISBN # Included?

5.   _____Bar Code Included?

6.   _____Online Sales? (Amazon, BN.com, Border)

7.   _____Available to order by Book Store?

8.   _____Book Store Returnable?

9.   _____Book Store Discount?

10. _____Custom Cover?

11. _____Cover Trade quality?

12. _____Authors Web Page?

13. _____Royalty Pay (quarterly, annual, monthly)

14. _____Royalty %

15. _____Proof ready when?

16. _____Proofing method (e-file, e-gallery, actual book)

17. _____Ability to check book status (24/7, N/A)

18. _____Author Discount?

19. _____**Author Book Signing Discount?**

20. _____**Author Support?** *(1 to 1, Phone, Rep. Assigned)*

21. _____**Free Books – How many if any?**

22. _____**Royalty w/ Author Purchase – terms?**

23. _____**Back Cover with picture?**

24. _____**Author Bio Length?**

25. _____**Book Order Delivery** (how long to arrive)

26. _____**Marketing Kit Available?**

27. _____**Other Promotional Material?**

28. _____**Copy Editing Service?**

29. _____**Quality Control?**

30. _____**Retain eBook Rights?** (sell ebook from web site?)

Bonus Report I

PROMOTE YOUR BOOK WITH BOOKLETS

When it comes to promoting your product or service business, most people think of the traditional marketing materials such as brochures, flyers, newsletters, and the like. Of course, these materials work just fine when written and designed properly, and targeted to the right market.

What most people don't consider and something you might after reading this is to use a simple booklet to promote your business. You may even want to produce an informative booklet to sell by itself or in a series. There are many reasons why you should consider booklets. Let's first explore the reasons why booklets can help you fatten your wallet!

One simple reason to consider a booklet: people are hungry for information and are willing to pay YOU good money for it! Now when I say they will pay you for information-packed booklets that help promote your business, service, or attract new associates to your networking sales organization, understand that your booklet does not always have to be sent to a prospect for FREE.

Rather, I suggest you consider a small fee or a regular retail price for two simple reasons: to build value and to weed out the freebie seekers that drain your resources. You will use the information your booklet provides to spell out in detail further information on your products or services! Yes, it's a DIFFERENT, and little-used marketing tool. But it works!

For example, a few days ago in my daily load of mail, I received a small booklet I'm looking at as I write this from my cluttered computer desk. This little booklet, essentially a 24-page pamphlet, is created by a well-known publisher of a wide variety of materials on multi-level marketing.

This simple booklet has been around for quite a few years and explains in the simplest of terms how multi-level marketing works. And although I received it for free (someone trying to recruit me into their MLM organization sent it along with other sales materials), most people will pay a small sum for it to send to potential prospects.

The writer/publisher gets more mileage out of this booklet than sales revenues alone. He is also seen as an expert is his field (MLM). And of course, this does a great deal to help his publishing and self-promotion efforts. This booklet, hence, serves a two-fold purpose: 1), it makes money off the initial sale (and includes an order form at the back to receive more of the publisher's offerings); and 2) The publisher is perceived as a knowledgeable resource on the booklet's subject.

You can see by this simple example that a booklet can help you promote just about any product or service, while making a tidy sum from the initial sale. And of course, I highly encourage you to publish one or even a series of booklets for an additional source of revenue to whatever products or services you market now. Self-published booklets can be a very profitable sideline business.

The added benefit of being perceived as an expert, or at least very knowledgeable on the subject of your booklet, will move your buyers to purchase more of your products or services from you in the future because they have in their hands a REAL, TANGIBLE product that you produced! Using a booklet to help promote your products or services is an UNUSUAL promotion method. Maybe you've never thought of using one.

Or maybe you've decided a brochure is the best way to spell out the benefits that your customers get when they choose you over your competitors. And don't get me wrong - I'm not saying to use a booklet instead of a brochure! If a brochure works for you, then stick with it.

For the most part, a brochure is a good choice when your products or services require a very short amount of detail to help "close" a prospect. Consider a booklet when you want to cover a lot of ground, giving your prospect/buyer a fairly large amount of detail. Booklets can run just about any length - within reason - but be sure not to go overboard and add to your prospect's information overload! Usually, 8 to 12 pages will do the job nicely.

For instance, two clients of mine (partners) came to me recently asking to evaluate the booklet they use to recruit prospects into their MLM organization. The 8 1/2 x 11 booklets contained a great deal of information - 16 solid pages!

The booklet explained their program in great detail, allowing for their potential new distributor to make a decision whether to sign up with them or not, based entirely on the information packed into their 8 1/2 x 11 booklet. I suggested that an edited version might work better. Too much information can bog down your prospect. Be careful not to overwhelm your already-too-busy prospect with too much material.

If you haven't considered a simple booklet to help promote your products or services while bringing in additional income _ maybe it's time to include one in your marketing plan! The exciting thing about booklets is their ability to promote just about any product, service, or organization you're involved with.

I have given several thousand of them away in various promotions throughout the years _ plus, you'll make a tidy profit from selling them, as well. Don't hesitate to give them a try -- trust me, booklets can give you the boost you're looking for!

SIMPLE MONEY MAKERS - TIPS BOOKLETS

How many times have you recited the same material to your clients, prospects, and audiences? Your elevator speech has become your grocery store and cleaners stop speech. Now imagine generating money directly from those same mini-billboards, from those pearls of wisdom that you turn on and off like a water faucet. Yes, it is possible, and here's how you do it.

Begin to jot those tidbits of information down as soon as they come to mind. Put them in a notebook or type them into a Word document. Don't worry about format just get them down, with just enough information to jog your memory about what you mean. You can edit them and arrange them later.

Let a couple weeks go by, allowing most of the information to surface in your thoughts. Rarely will it happen by taking two hours on a Saturday afternoon to sit at your computer to think of it all.

Weed out and organize the tips. Divide them into categories and edit the text. Use a writing style similar to what you are reading here.

Be sure to include your contact details so readers can easily reach you. Add a brief section about your background so people will know your qualifications for presenting the information.

Hire a graphic designer to make the words look good on the page. Your completed product will be a tips booklet measuring about 3 ½ inches by 8 ½ inches when printed. The designer will create their part of the finished product as a PDF file.

Send the PDF file from your graphic designer to a printing company. Do an initial print run of 1,000 copies. Think about who can benefit from using your booklet to promote their own product, service, or cause. Send them a sample of your booklet and a cover letter describing some of the ways they can increase their sales or further their cause by using your booklet as a promotional tool.

Consider corporations, associations, publications, and any other group that seems appropriate for the topic of your booklet. Reach out to as many of them as you can, on whatever budget of time and money you have available to you.

Realize that every time one of the large-quantity buyers sends out your booklet to promote their own product, service, or cause, they are also marketing your business. Your contact information in the booklet allows the reader to reach you directly.

Enjoy the expansion of your customer base and your checking account. You are now reaching a larger audience than you are likely to do single-handedly, thanks to the large-quantity buyers of your booklet. And you have been paid by your buyers to reach those new people.

Those sound bites you have been saying for years are now reaching far beyond your current clients, helping your buyers, their clients, and your own business. It doesn't get a lot better than getting paid for your marketing materials.

QUICK START GUIDE: FIVE TIPS TO ACTUALLY DO A BOOKLET

Now it's time to look at the delivery of that material. Consider the following things about size that can make a huge difference in the success of your booklet:

Run of copy - Present your content in short, pointed, 'bullet' format. Write your copy as tips instead of as long narrative. Less is more. Your readers will be drawn to the material faster when it is presented as 'sound bites' rather than paragraphs. Group the tips in sub-categories of 10-12 tips so the reader sees small, approachable groups of information as they open any page of the booklet.

Type size - Use a type size that accommodates the ever-increasing numbers of Baby Boomers who now reach for their reading glasses. A small type size can be an instant discouragement to someone who would find your material to be just what they need.

Dimensions - Create your booklet to be approximately 3.5" x 8.5", fitting into a #10 size business envelope. That size is vastly more flexible for selling both single copies and large quantities. It is far superior to 5.5" x 8.5" (catalog size), in use, production, and shipping costs.

Number of pages - Keep your booklet in the range of 16-20 interior pages, with a maximum of 24 pages if you really must. This is not The Great American Novel. It is an informational booklet. Consider doing a second booklet to include whatever material that couldn't fit into the pages of the first booklet.

Print quantity - Do a first print run of 500-1000 copies. A print run of that size provides you an adequate quantity for on-hand inventory to fill orders. It also gives you a good number to send out as samples to publications to excerpt from your booklet, and samples to prospective large quantity buyers. Keep your first print run to this size so you can make any corrections that slip past even the best proof readers.

By considering size in these ways, you will go a long way to positively impacting the size of some other things: the contribution you make to other people's lives AND the size of your checkbook balance!

SUMMARY

Now you have a money-making tips booklet that has the potential of spreading the word about your book and making extra money for you as well. If you are a good typist, go ahead and type it out in finished form. If you're not a typist, you can have it typed by someone who is, or even have it typeset for a small fee. Whatever you write about, make it something you know about.

Bonus Report II

UNLOCK THE DOOR TO SUCCESS WITH PROFITABLE ADS

The success of your advertising will ultimately depend on the salability of your book, manual, report, newsletter, etc. Good advertising will make a good book sell better, but it cannot transform a poor book into being successful.

Advertising is vital to any business venture because:
- It allows a business to deliver their message repeatedly and reinforce it in the minds of targeted consumers.
- It allows a business to reach hundreds of thousands of potential customers at a relatively low cost compared to individual calls.
- It allows a business to target their market and test their product.
- A business identity can quickly be established.
- A forum for showing a product, together with benefits and advantages can be established.

BASIC ADVERTISING RULES

Effective marketing is a vast field. It includes using marketing tools such as: direct mail; space and classified ads; signs; radio and TV commercials; business involvement, and more. In fact, the approaches you can take and the methods you use are only limited by your imagination and resources. There are basic rules however that do not change however. They are as follows:

Rule No. 1-You must get a prospects ATTENTION. (Your headline is the most important part of an advertisement.)

Rule No. 2-You must create reader INTEREST (Your ad should be built around an idea that offers value.)

Rule No. 3-You must arouse the reader's DESIRE. (By focusing on all the benefits they will receive.)

Rule No. 4-Your ad must move them to ACT. (Tell your readers exactly what it is you what them to do.)

In order to avoid making careless advertising decisions that can cost you money, it is important that you understand and participate in your own strategies. That means getting involved and researching what strategy will produce sound advertising. It is essential that you have a plan before you take action on developing advertising strategy.

Your plan must be based on an objective analysis that resulted from your knowledge and it doesn't matter what your background is, you can learn to master the type of mail order advertising that is needed to launch a self-publishing business.

Through research and careful planning you can become familiar with the writing skills you will need to create effective ads. Obtain all the information you can from the masters in the business.

Read and study every book, manual, report, newsletter, sales letter, ad, article, and publication you can get your hands on that will help you in developing your own successful strategies and techniques. Then bring all of that knowledge together to obtain winning results.

The art of advertising is only slightly different from the brochure. In a brochure, you have more time and space to put your message across. In advertising, only a few words are used. Advertisements must stop the reader and thus need a "grabber" headline.

You must always remember the purpose of the advertisement. It's not to SELL anyone, but to attract enough INTEREST to get the person to call for more information. Then the real selling can start!

There are words that are consistently effective in pulling in an audience and initiating a response. Here's a short-list:

amazing	profitable
easy	secret
free	simple

now	privileged
special offer	win
incredible	don't wait
make money	startling

Businesses need to attract clients. Advertising will do that if it's done well. This is where you come in. Read advertisements! Which ones do you respond best to? Try this: cut out a few of the advertisements you like best and show them to several friends. Record their level of interest and rank the results.

You'll probably see a pattern where one or two of the advertisements emerge at the top of everyone's list. Study those to see why. Very likely, you'll see that the use of a few key words and the message they imply will prompt people to respond positively to those ads.

Bonus Reports III

HOW TO WRITE AND SUBMIT
A POWER PACKED PRESS RELEASE

The word "Press Release" seems to scare most people to death. On top of that -- not many people take the time to even think of writing their own Press Release. We hope this brief article will help clear up some of the mystery's surrounding this simple form of marketing.

The first thing you have to remember is that a Press Release is a "news" item. It exists to "inform" people, NOT sell them something. For example, you are reading this report because you want to learn something that will BENEFIT YOU. You aren't reading it just so you can buy something else.

If money is the driving force in your business -- you won't go too far. Your main goals should be in pleasing customers, providing them with a high-quality product and more than their money's worth. The trick is to do all this while still making money.

People don't care what mountains you had to climb, what seas you had to cross or what tribe of people you had to learn the ways of just to find a secret formula. Instead -- they want to know WHAT the secret formula is and WHAT it can do for them. Get the idea?

The sales circulars you print and mail sell your product. A Press Release informs others about your product. Instead of your main objective being to sell the product and have the customer send in an order immediately, a Press Release informs the customer exactly how your product will benefit their lives.

This must be conveyed in the form of a "newsworthy" Press Release. If you have a sales circular to sell a product, you can easily turn it into a Press Release without much difficulty. It's just a new marketing angle of presenting your product to the public.

Press releases are one of the most cost-effective ways to get promotion for your book online. Many authors and small business owners alike ignore this type of promotion because they don't know how to write a press release. It's important to promote your book with press releases because of the media all over the internet. The following is a list of some common press release writing tips:

- your press release should sound like news, not an ad
- you should only send your press release to the media related to the topic of your press release
- keep your press release one page in length
- your header, contact information and release date should be at the top of your press release
- use short sentences and double space in between sentences
- your header and first few sentences should capture the readers attention
- you should tell a story and briefly mention your business, product or service in the body of the press release
- ➢ proofread your press release many times. Look for grammar and spelling mistakes.

Another reason entrepreneurs ignore promoting their online business with press releases is because they don't know what's newsworthy. Here are 16 online business press release ideas:

- new products (book) or services you're offering on your web site.
- the results of an online survey or poll you've completed
- a virtual trade show or seminar you're hosting.
- a free chat room class you're teaching
- your opening of a new web site
- an online award your business or web site has won
- a free e-mail newsletter you're publishing

- new online products or services you're giving away
- an online business association or club you're starting
- a famous person that's endorsing your business
- a major joint venture you're doing with another business
- a new book or e-book you wrote
- an expert or celebrity who's speaking in your chat room
- a fundraising event you're doing at your web site
- a new contest or sweepstakes you're having at your site
- major sponsorships you're doing online

The following is sample copy from a typical Press Release for publishing services:

So many people are entering the mail order market these days, but so many of them are getting ripped-off by a bunch of hype. People are promised untold riches in a short period of time. The hype ads play with their emotions by making them believe it's so easy to make money through the mail. It's sad.

However, a new book has just been released to help solve these problems for the average person. For the first time in history -- a REAL directory has been compiled listing the ACTUAL name and addresses of 179 honest and trustworthy mail order folks. People can write DIRECTLY to these people and receive FREE information to get them started in their own business now!

It's unbelievable. Without trying to sell you anything else, you can get this book for only $4.95 -- a price anyone can afford. Meet the real mail order dealers who care about their products and want to help you get started doing what they are doing.

Only available from Graphico Publishing, PO Box 488, Bluff City TN 37618.

As you can see, this is a short but sweet Press Release -- however, you should be able to see the "newsworthiness" in it. It's main focus is on the fact that most people get ripped-off when they start their first mail order business.

The solution to this problem is a new directory that is available for the first time in history. The sell is slowly led into because the reader will naturally want to get their hands on this one. It doesn't ask for money -- it only tells the reader how to get a copy if they want one.

Here's a great test for a real press release. Since your final sales pitch is included in the last paragraph -- read the Press Release aloud. Would it still be worth reading WITHOUT your sales pitch? If so, it's probably a Press Release.

Press Releases come in many forms due to the product you are writing about. However, the basic rule of thumb still applies. If you've never written one before -- it may be a little difficult.

Don't despair. Grab the latest daily newspaper and read some of their informational articles. Notice how each article is written and pattern yours after the same format. After you do a few of them -- you'll be able to "get the picture."

When your Press Release is written to your satisfaction, the proper way to submit it to a publisher is:

- Be sure and type it on a typewriter or computer.
- Standard format is double-spaced and not longer than two 8 1/2x11 pages.
- Be sure and put your name, address and page number at the top of each page.
- Write the words: "For Immediate Release." at the top.

If you are only sending the press release to one publication -- tell them it's a "first run."

Summary
You can get other press release writing tips and ideas by reading other businesses press releases, reading how to publications, talking to experts and visiting other media
web sites. I hope this chapter persuades and helps you to promote your book through press releases.

Press Release Template

Here is a sample press release template for you to use if you wish. Feel free to edit it any way you wish to suit your own purposes.

FOR IMMEDIATE RELEASE

Headline

<Insert your headline. Remember – this is what people will see first so make it a good one>

Summary

<Insert a brief lead-in paragraph>

Main text

<Now insert the main body of your press release. Refer to the guidance tips in the ebook for assistance>

Contact details

<How can people contact you if they wish to>

Company/personal information

<A brief paragraph about yourself, your company, your web site>

EARMA BROWN

Bonus Report IV

HOW TO WRITE PROFITABLE CLASSIFIED ADS

Everybody wants to make more money... In fact, most people would like to hit upon something that makes them fabulously rich! And seemingly, (at the time of this writing) one of the easiest roads to the fulfillment of these dreams of wealth is publishing or within the professional circles of the business, publishing or Internet selling...

The only thing is, hardly anyone gives much real thought to still one of the basic ingredients of selling their product - the writing of profitable classified ads. If your book or publishing venture is to succeed, then you must acquire the expertise of writing classified ads that sell your product or services!

So what makes a classified ad good or bad? First of all, it must appeal to the reader, and as such, it must say exactly what you want it to say. Secondly, it has to say what it says in the least possible number of words in order to keep your operating costs within your budget. And thirdly, it has to produce the desired results whether inquiries or sales.

Grabbing the reader's attention is your first objective. You must assume the reader is "scanning" the page on which your ad appears in the company of two or three hundred classified ads. Therefore, there has to be something about your ad that causes him to stop scanning and look at yours! So, the first two or three words of your ad are of the utmost importance and deserve your careful consideration. Most surveys show that words or phrases that quickly involve the reader, tend to be the best attention-grabbers. Such words as: FREE... WIN... MAKE BIG MONEY...

Whatever words you use as attention-grabbers, to start your ads, you should bear in mind that they'll be competing with similar attention-grabbers of the other ads on the same page.

Therefore, in addition to your lead words, your ad must quickly go on to promise or state further benefits to the reader. In other words, your ad might read something like this: MAKE BIG MONEY! Easy & Simple. We show you how!

In the language of professional copywriters, you've grabbed the attention of your prospect, and interested him with something that even he can do.

The next rule of good classified copywriting has to do with the arousal of the reader's desire to get in on your offer. In a great many instances, this rule is by-passed, and it appears, this is the real reason that an ad doesn't pull according to the expectations of the advertiser.

Think about it - you've got your reader's attention; you've told him it's easy and simple; and you're about to ask him to do something. Unless you take the time to further "want your offer," your ad is going to only half turn him on. He'll compare your ad with the others that have grabbed his attention and finally decide upon the one that interests him the most.

What I'm saying is that here is the place for you to insert that magic word "guaranteed" or some other such word or phrase. So now, we've got an ad that reads: MAKE BIG MONEY! Easy & Simple. Guaranteed!

Now the reader is turned on, and in his mind, he can't lose. You're ready to ask for his money. This is the "demand for action" part of your ad. This is the part where you want to use such words as: Limited offer - Act now! Write today! Only and/or just...

Putting it all together, then your ad might read something like this: MAKE BIG MONEY! Easy & Simple. Guaranteed! Limited offer. Send $1 to:

These are the ingredients of any good classified ad - Attention - Interest - Desire - Action... Without these four ingredients skillfully integrated into your ad, chances are your ad will just "lie there" and not do anything but cost you money. What we've just shown you is a basic classified ad. Although such an ad could be placed in any leading publication and would pull a good response, it's known as a "blind ad" and would pull inquiries and responses from a whole spectrum of people reading the publication in which it appeared. In other words, from as many "time-wasters" as from bona fide buyers.

So let's try to give you an example of the kind of classified ad you might want to use, say to sell a report such as this one... Using all the rules of basic advertising copywriting, and stating exactly what our product is, our ad reads thusly:

> *MONEY-MAKER'S SECRETS! How To Write winning classified ads. Simple & easy to learn -should double or triple your responses. Rush $1 to BC Sales, 10 Main Anytown, TX 75001.*

The point we're making is that: 1) You've got to grab the reader's attention... 2) You've got to "interest him" with something that appeals to him... 3) You've got to "further stimulate" him with something (catch-phrase) that makes him "desire" the product or service... 4) Demand that he act immediately...

There's no point in being tricky or clever. Just adhere to the basics and your profits will increase accordingly. One of the best ways of learning to write good classified ads is to study the classifieds - try to figure out exactly what they're attempting to sell - and then practice rewriting them according to the rules we've just given you. Whenever you sit down to write a classified, always write it all out - write down everything you want to say - and then go back over it, crossing out words, and refining your phraseology.

The final ingredient of your classified ad is of course, your name, address to which the reader is to respond - where he's to send his money or write for further information.

Generally speaking, readers respond more often to ads that include a name than to those showing just initials or an address only. However, because advertising costs are based upon the number of words, or the amount of space your ad uses, the use of some names in classified ads could become quite expensive.

If we were to ask our ad respondents to write to or send their money to The Research Writers & Publishers Association, or to Book Business Mart, or even to Money Maker's Opportunity Digest, our advertising costs would be prohibitive. Thus we shorten our name Researchers or Money-Makers. The point here is to think relative to the placement costs of your ad, and to shorten excessively long names.

The same holds true when listing your post office box number. Shorten it to just plain Box 40, or in the case of a rural delivery, shorten it to just RR1.

The important thing is to know the rules of profitable classified ad writing, and to follow them. Hold your costs in line.

Now you know the basics... the rest is up to your ads.

RESOURCE SECTION

BUTTERFLY PRESS
Imagine finally connecting with a publishing company who takes your message seriously. You can now realize the dream that has been inside you for (it seems like forever) a very long time.

Butterfly Press will work with you to breathe life into your dream of publishing a book.

Butterfly Press is committed to helping others dream a bigger dream in writing, book development and publishing. Seeking to supply excellent written material that will instruct, inspire, encourage and elevate those who read the pages of the books from Butterfly Press for generations to come.

Butterflies are symbolic of transformations, emergence and victories won. They represent the very essence of change, creativity and then pollinating to share it with the world. Visit *Butterfly Press* today! **http://butterflypress.net**

INNER COURT PUBLISHING (CHRISTIAN BOOKS)
an imprint of Butterfly press
http://innercourtpublishing.com

100 DAYS TO A BOOK
Sign up today for the 12 Week Book Writing Course and uncover the best way to get your wildly successful book written fast! For all the details on a proven program that walks you through 12 amazingly simple lessons to get your book written and out to the world. Now is better than later. Visit us at http://bookwritingcourse.com for the 100 Days To a Book course.

Ebook It! How to Profit From Your Passion with Ebooks
Are you looking for a way to turn your knowledge into a profit center? Creating an ebook using your information is the fastest and most profitable way to make money online.
http://www.ebookitsuccess.com

Write to Win Affiliates

Sell Earma's Book Writing, Marketing and Publishing Ebooks on your website to make extra cash! http://www.writetowin.net

40+ Article Writing Templates

Article Writing Templates - 40 easy Article Writing Templates from author Earma Brown! The templates offer you a jumpstart on writing short easy articles fast. Also, these are the same templates Earma uses to promote her products and services to profit every week. Visit this website for details and download your set of templates: http://www.40articlewritingtemplates.com

READY FOR THE NEXT LEVEL VISIT THE iWIN NETWORK?

Visit the iWIN network and discover how to use YOUR information to write books, create products and grow your own profit stream. Learn how to tap into your inner creativity, create connection with other writers and build community! Like us on Facebook and receive a free iWIN Success Screensaver.

International Writers Information Network (Membership)

http://writersinformationnetwork.com

iWIN Community

http://iwinontheweb.com

Write to Win Institute

http://writetowin.org

Write to Win Affiliates

http://writetowin.net

RESOURCE ROLODEX

1. **Free Way to Create Ebook:**
   http://cutepdf.com/Products/CutePDF/Writer.asp

2. **Ebook Creator Software**
   http://www.writetowin.net/products/eWriter-Pro-Software.html

3. **Free Way to Create & Record Audio version product:**
   http://audacity.sourceforge.net/

4. **Free Way to do interview with experts in your field.**
   http://www.gizmoproject.com

5. **Free Online Teleprompter for creating Podcast**
   http://www.cueprompter.com/

6. **Free Way to Create Membership Site**
   http://opensourcecms.com/

7. **Publish Your Own (Physical) book for less than $10**
   http://www.lulu.com

8. **Publish Your Own (Physical) book or product for FREE setup or sign up for pro account using less than $50**
   http://www.createspace.com

9. **Book Cover Software**
   http://www.bookcoverpro.com

10. **Book Layout Software (Book Design Wizard)**
    http://www.self-pub.net/wizard.html

11. **Open source office suite (like MS Office)**
    http://www.openoffice.org/

ABOUT THE AUTHOR

Earma Brown lives in Northern Texas with husband Varn. She is an author, publisher and book coach strategist who teaches entrepreneurs, teachers, coaches and infopreneurs how to put their core message into a saleable book. Earma has a Bachelor's degree in Business. Author of twelve books, Earma's expertise has been shared in five writing and publishing helps books and hundreds of expert articles. Using her signature *Write to Win* products and *iWIN* programs, Earma's clients learn how to transform their original works into multiple products and services.

www.ingramcontent.com/pod-product-compliance
Lightning Source LLC
Chambersburg PA
CBHW031507270326
41930CB00006B/295